Routledge Revivals

THE BOOK OF THE DEAD

EGYPTIAN HIEROGLYPHIC TEXT

Books on Egypt and Chaldaea

THE CHAPTERS

OF

COMING FORTH BY DAY

OR

THE THEBAN RECENSION

OF THE

BOOK OF THE DEAD

THE EGYPTIAN HIEROGLYPHIC TEXT EDITED
FROM NUMEROUS PAPYRI

BY

E. A. WALLIS BUDGE, M. A., LITT. D., D. LITT., D. LIT.
KEEPER OF THE EGYPTIAN AND ASSYRIAN ANTIQUITIES
IN THE BRITISH MUSEUM

Routledge
Taylor & Francis Group

First published in 1910 by Kegan Paul, Trench, Trubner & Co. Ltd.

This edition first published in 2018 by Routledge
2 Park Square, Milton Park, Abingdon, Oxon, OX14 4RN
and by Routledge
711 Third Avenue, New York, NY 10017

Routledge is an imprint of the Taylor & Francis Group, an informa business

Publisher's Note
The publisher has gone to great lengths to ensure the quality of this reprint but points out that some imperfections in the original copies may be apparent.

Disclaimer
The publisher has made every effort to trace copyright holders and welcomes correspondence from those they have been unable to contact.
A Library of Congress record exists under ISBN: 02021964

ISBN 13: 978-1-138-55400-9 (hbk)
ISBN 13: 978-1-138-56725-2 (pbk)
ISBN 13: 978-1-315-12417-9 (ebk)

Books on Egypt and Chaldaea

Vol. XXX of the Series

THE BOOK OF THE DEAD

EGYPTIAN HIEROGLYPHIC TEXT

Vol. III

CHAPTERS CLIII—CXC AND APPENDICES

Books on Egypt and Chaldaea

THE CHAPTERS OF COMING FORTH BY DAY OR THE THEBAN RECENSION OF THE BOOK OF THE DEAD

THE EGYPTIAN HIEROGLYPHIC TEXT EDITED FROM NUMEROUS PAPYRI

BY

E. A. WALLIS BUDGE, M. A., LITT. D., D. LITT., D. LIT.
KEEPER OF THE EGYPTIAN AND ASSYRIAN ANTIQUITIES
IN THE BRITISH MUSEUM

VOLUME III

CHAPTERS CLIII—CXC AND APPENDICES

LONDON
KEGAN PAUL, TRENCH, TRÜBNER & CO., LTD.
DRYDEN HOUSE, 43, GERRARD STREET, W.
1910

PRINTED BY
ADOLF HOLZHAUSEN,
19-21 KANDLGASSE, VIENNA.

THE CHAPTERS
OF
COMING FORTH BY DAY.

Chapter CLIII.

[A. From the Papyrus of Nu (Brit. Mus. No. 10,477, sheet 20).]
[B. From the Papyrus of Nu (Brit. Mus. No. 10,477, sheet 20).]

A

19
20
21
22
23
24
25
26

27
28
29
(?)
30
31
(?)
32

33 [hieroglyphs]

[hieroglyphs]

34 [hieroglyphs]

[hieroglyphs]

35 [hieroglyphs]

RUBRIC (Lepsius, *op. cit.*, p. 74): [hieroglyphs]

[hieroglyphs]

[hieroglyphs]

[hieroglyphs]

B 1 [hieroglyphs]

[hieroglyphs] 2 [hieroglyphs]

[hieroglyphs]

[hieroglyphs] 3 [hieroglyphs]

[hieroglyphs]

[hieroglyphs] 4 [hieroglyphs]

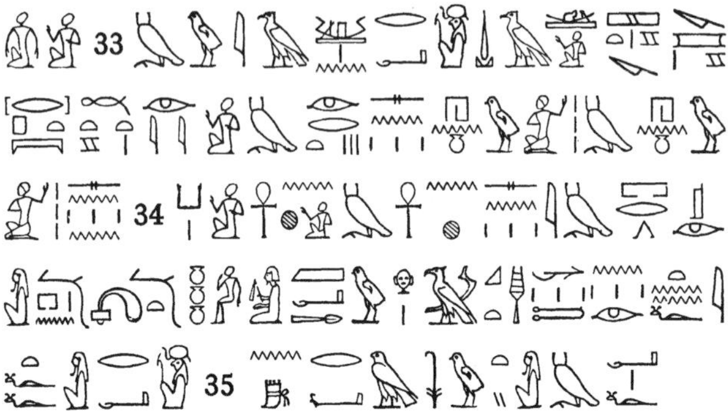

12
13
14
15
16
17
18

CHAPTER CLIV.

[A. From the Papyrus of Nu (Brit. Mus. No. 10,477, sheet 18).]
[B. From the Saïte Recension (Lepsius, *op. cit.*, Plate 75).]

13
14
15
16
17
18
19

20
21
B
1
2
3
4
5

6
7
8
9
10

CHAPTER CLV.

[A. From the Papyrus of Nu (Brit. Mus. No. 10,477, sheet 27).]
[B. From the Papyrus of Iuåu (ed. Naville, plate 13).]
[C. Rubric from the Saïte Recension (Lepsius, *op. cit.*, plate 75).]

A 1 

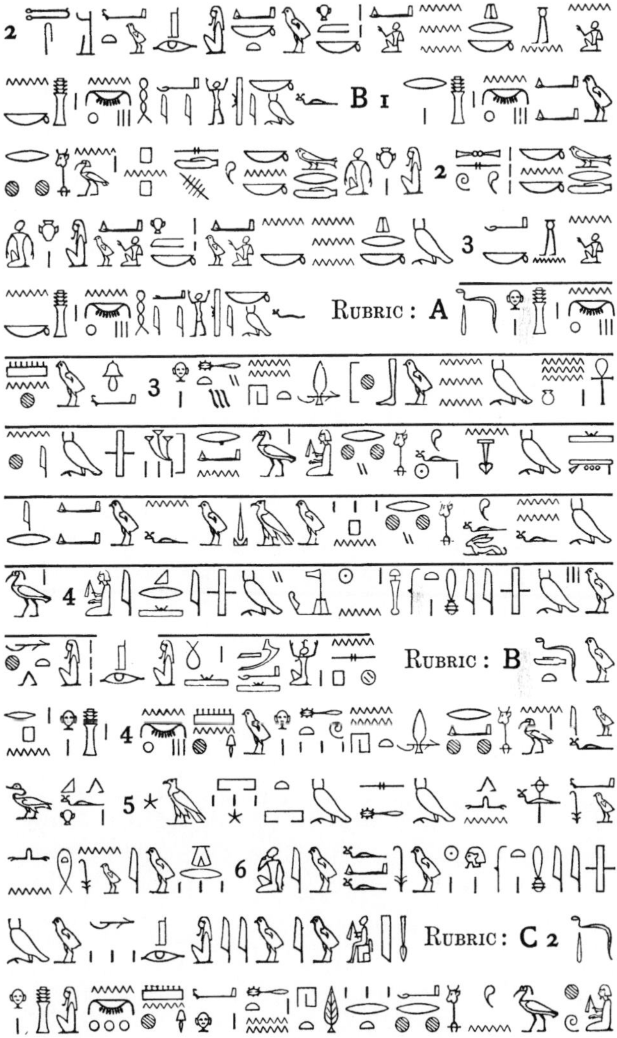
2
B I
2
3
Rubric : A
3
4
Rubric : B
4
5
6
Rubric : C 2

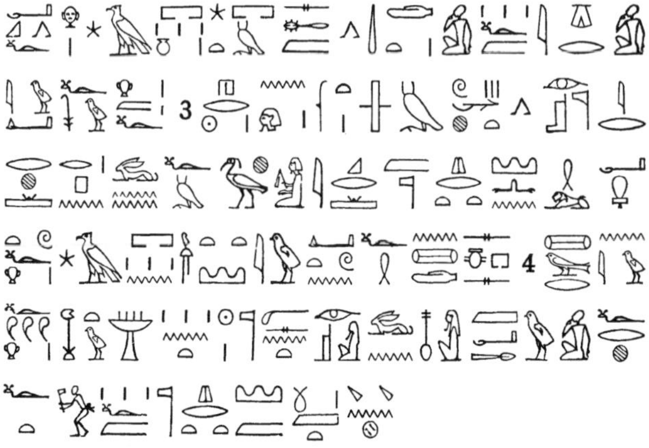

CHAPTER CLVI.

[A. From the Papyrus of Nu (Brit. Mus. No. 10,477, sheet 27).]
[B. From the Papyrus of Iuåu (ed. Naville, plate 13).]
[C. Rubric from the Saïte Recension (Lepsius, *op. cit.*, plate 75).]

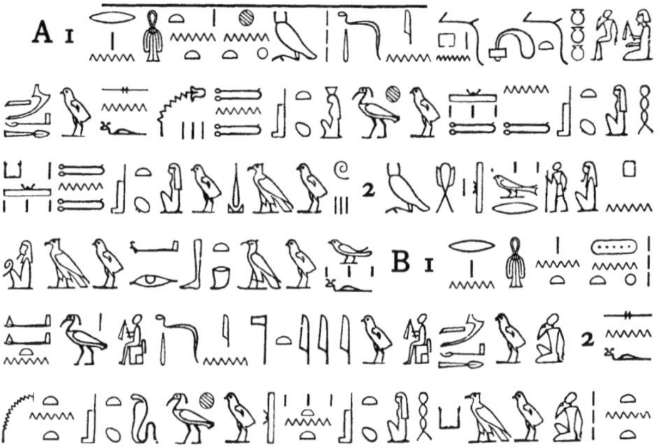

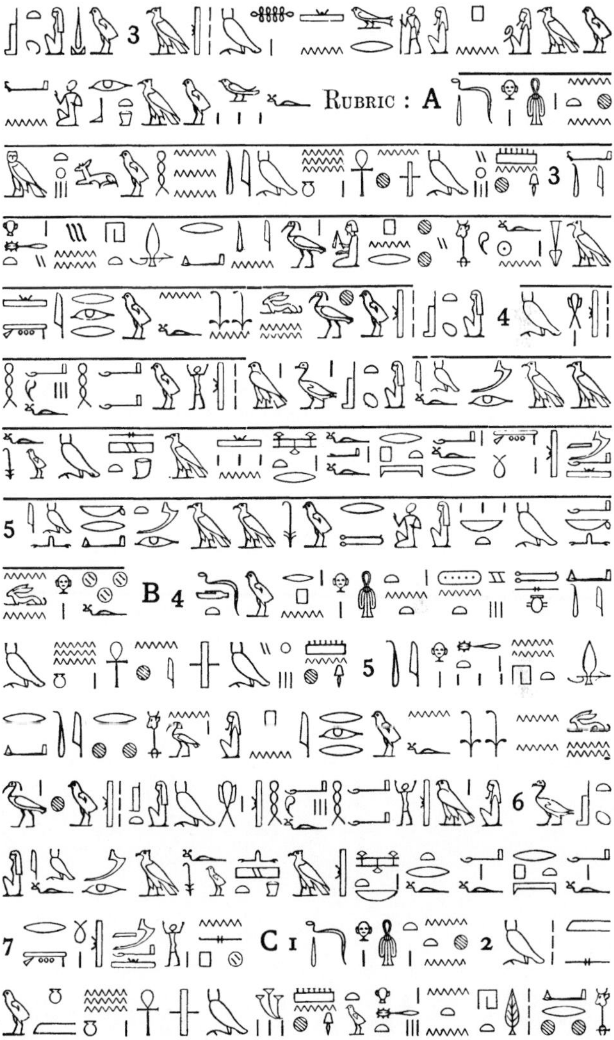
3
Rubric : A
3
4
5
B 4
5
6
7
C 1
2

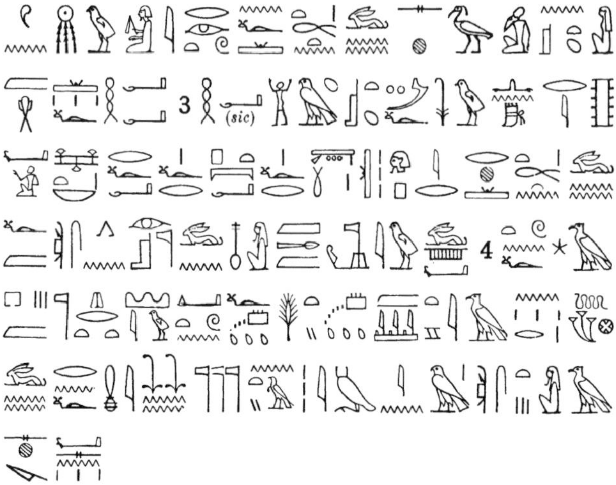

CHAPTER CLVII.

[From Lepsius, *Todtenbuch*, plate 76.]

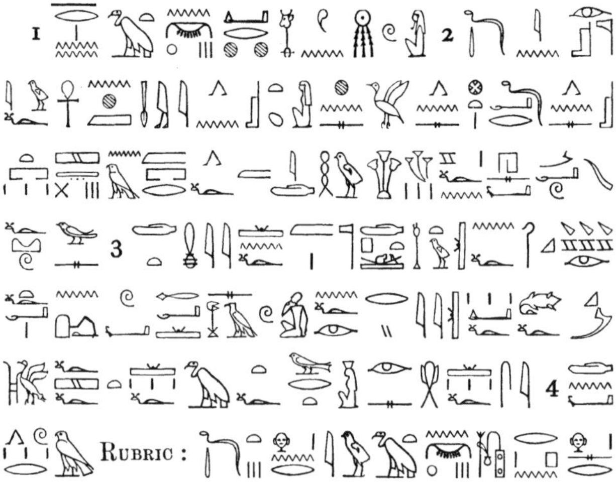

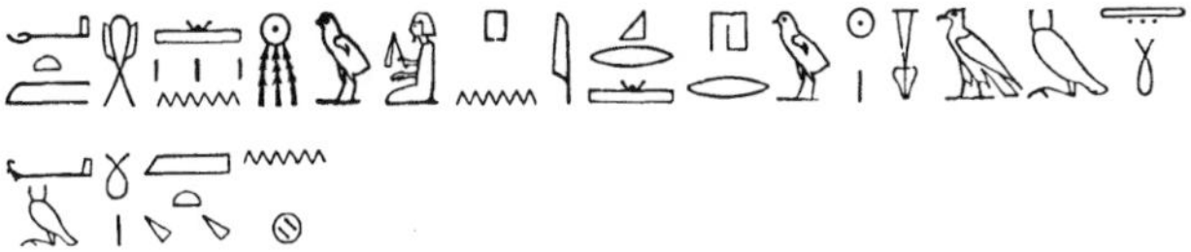

CHAPTER CLVIII.

[From Lepsius, *Todtenbuch*, plate 76.]

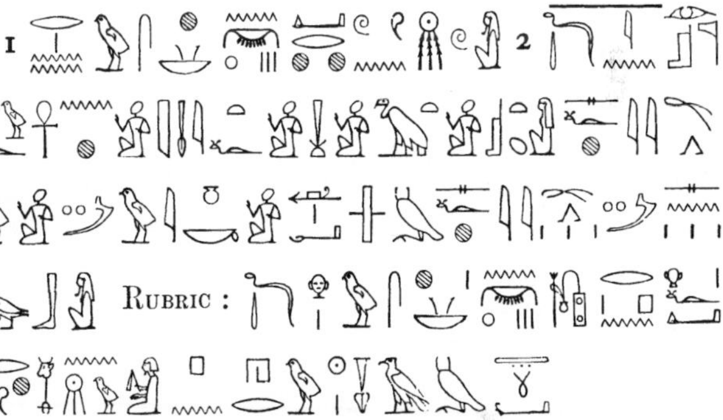

CHAPTER CLIX.

[From Lepsius, *Todtenbuch*, pl. 76.]

Chapter CLX.

[From the Papyrus of Nebseni (Brit. Mus. No. 9,900, sheet 10).]

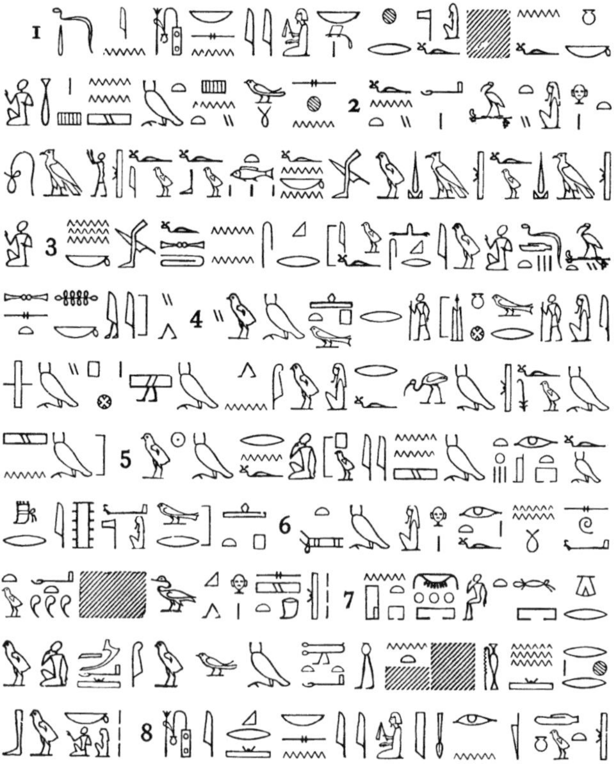

CHAPTER CLXI.

[From the Papyrus of Nefer-uben-f (Naville, *op. cit.*, Bd. 1, Bl. 184).]

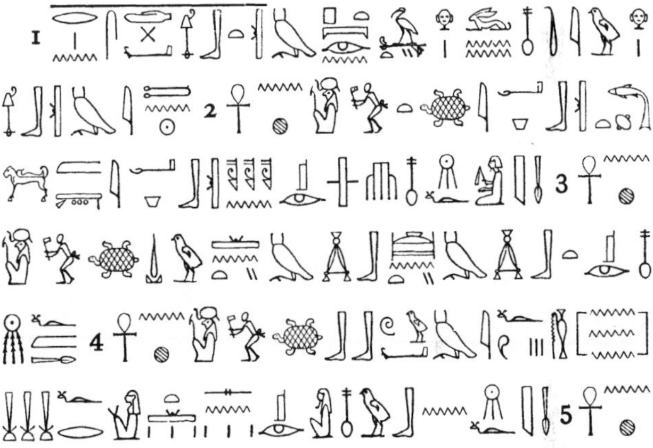

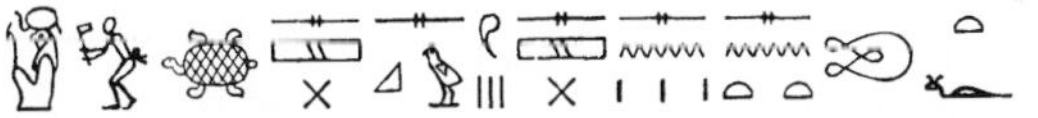

RUBRIC:

From the Saïte Recension

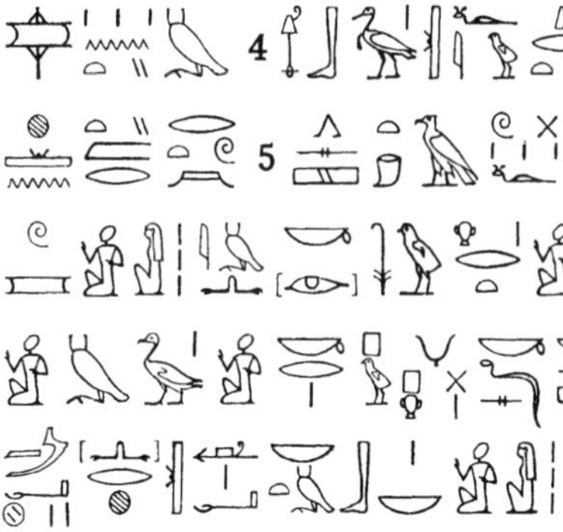

CHAPTER CLXII.

[From Lepsius, *Todtenbuch*, pl. 77.]

4
5
6
7
8
RUBRIC :
9

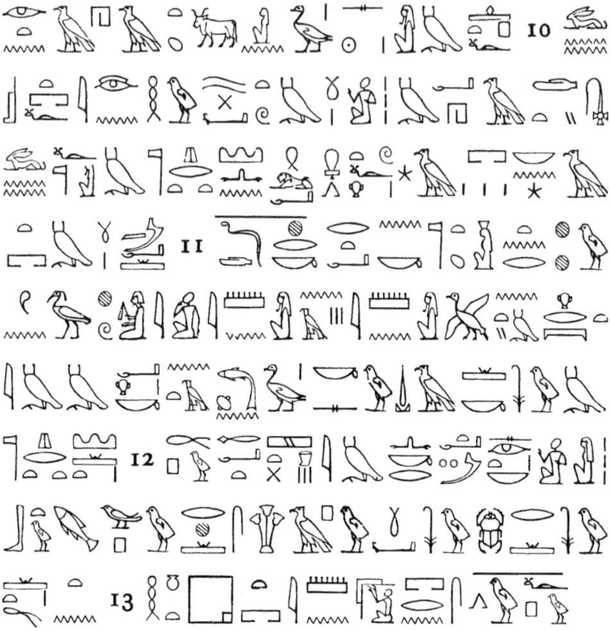

CHAPTER CLXIII.

[From Lepsius, *Todtenbuch*, pl. 77.]

13
RUBRIC:
14
15
16
17
18

CHAPTER CLXIV.

[From Lepsius, *Todtenbuch*, pl. 78.]

RUBRIC: 12

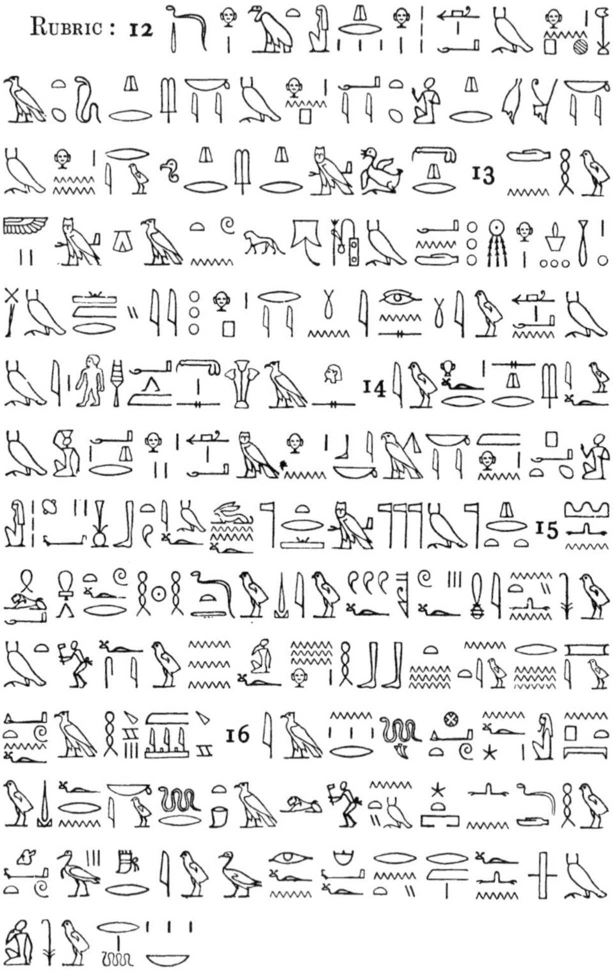

CHAPTER CLXV.

[From Lepsius, *Todtenbuch*, pl. 79.]

7
8
9
10
11
RUBRIC :
12
13

CHAPTER CLXVI.

[From the Papyrus of Nebseni (Brit. Mus. No. 9,900, sheet 21).]

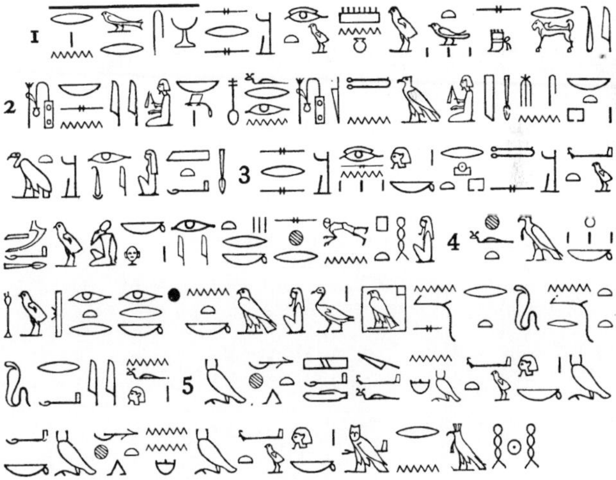

CHAPTER CLXVII.

[From the Papyrus of Nebseni (Brit. Mus. No. 9,900, sheet 22).]

CHAPTER CLXVIII.

[A. From the Papyrus of Mut-ḥetep (Brit. Mus. No. 10,010, sheet 2).]
[B. From Papyrus Brit. Mus. No. 10,478, sheets 2—7.]

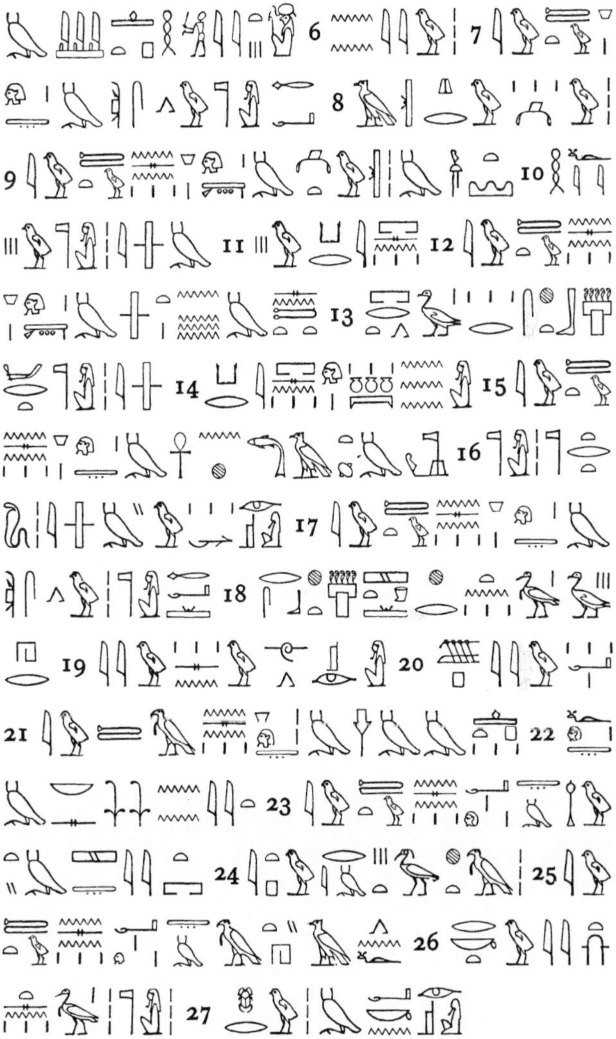

B I.

II.

III.

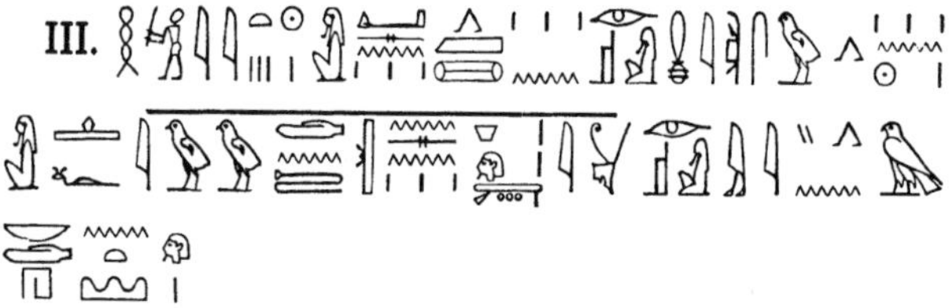

IV.

V.

1. The name of the deceased is omitted throughout the papyrus.

VI. 

VII. 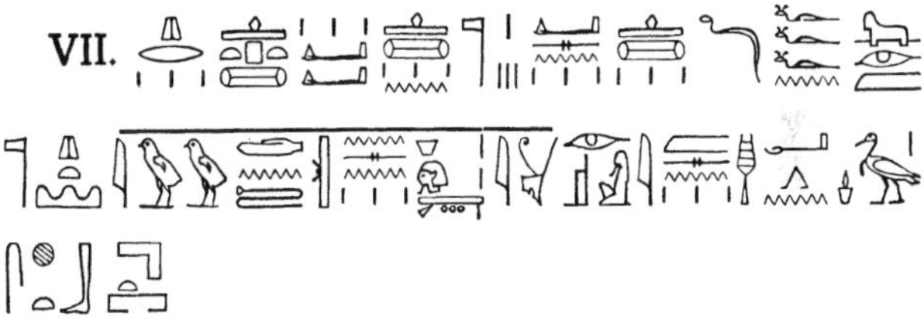

I. 

II. 

III. 

IV.

V.

VI.

VII.

VIII.

IX.

X.

XI.

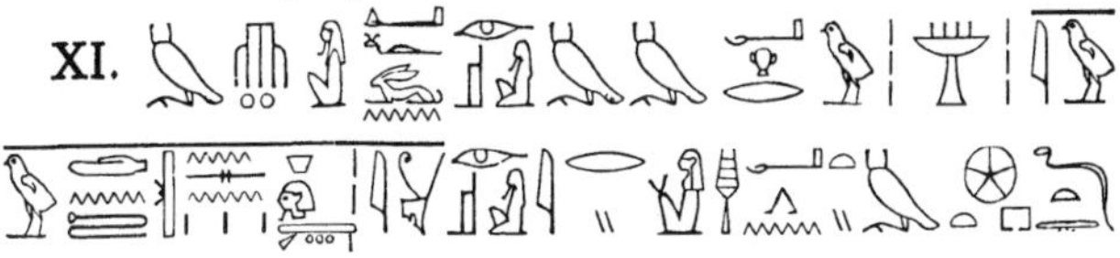

XII.

XIII.

XIV.

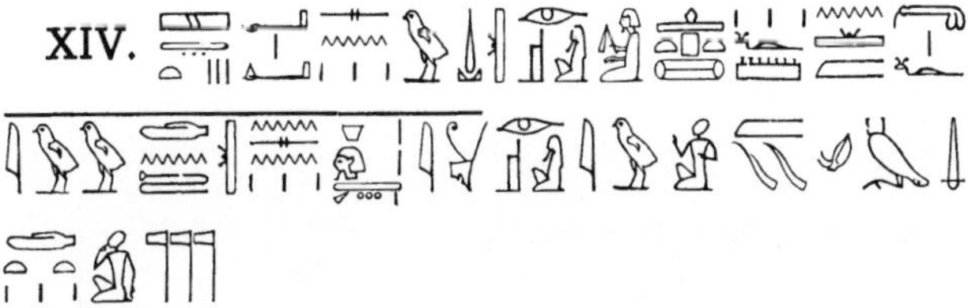

XV.

XVI. 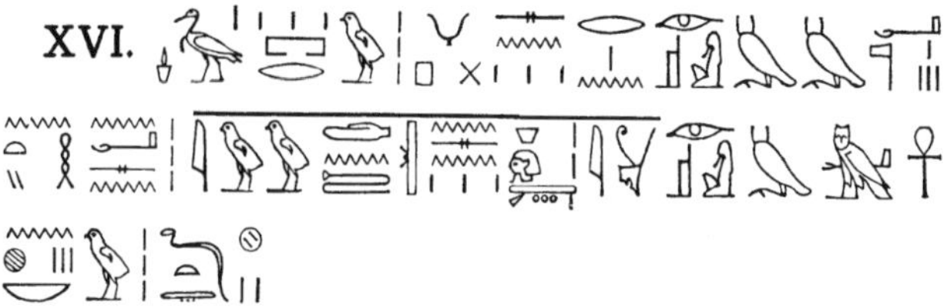

XVII. 

XVIII. 

XIX. 

XX. 

I. 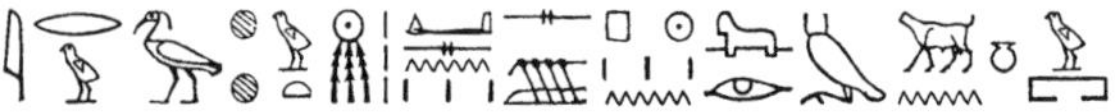

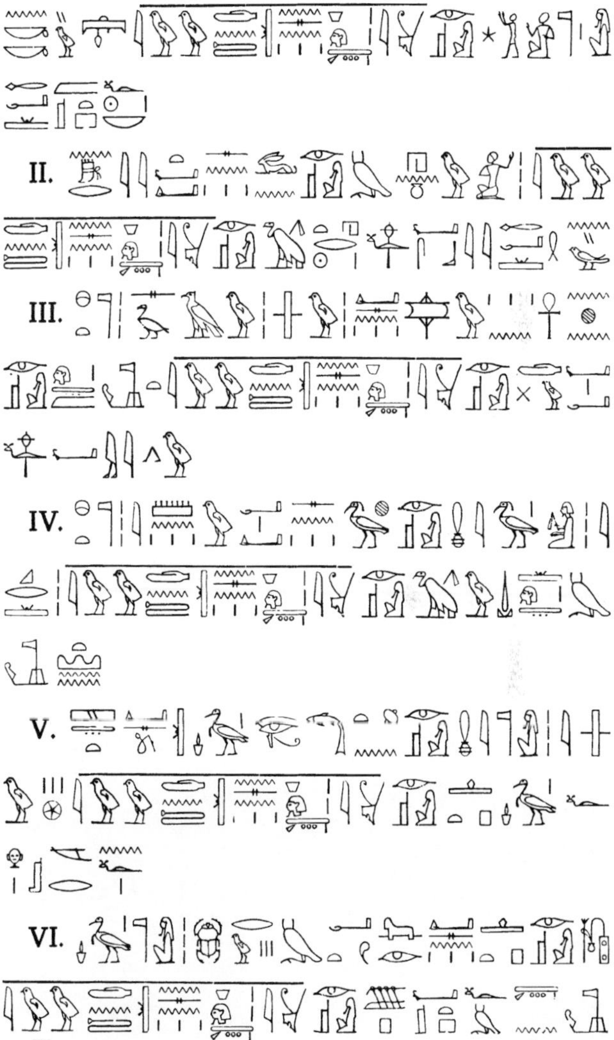
II.
III.
IV.
V.
VI.

VII.

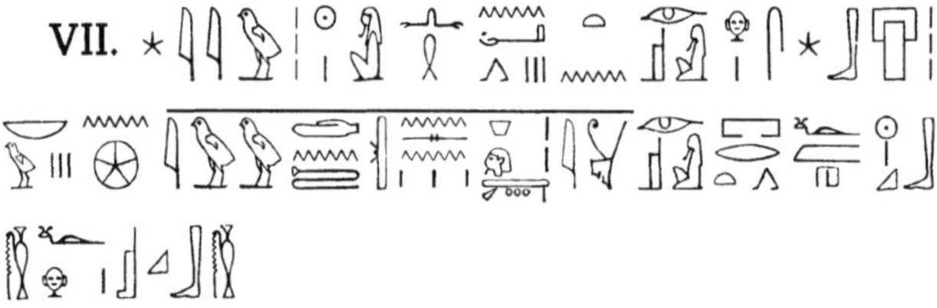

VIII.

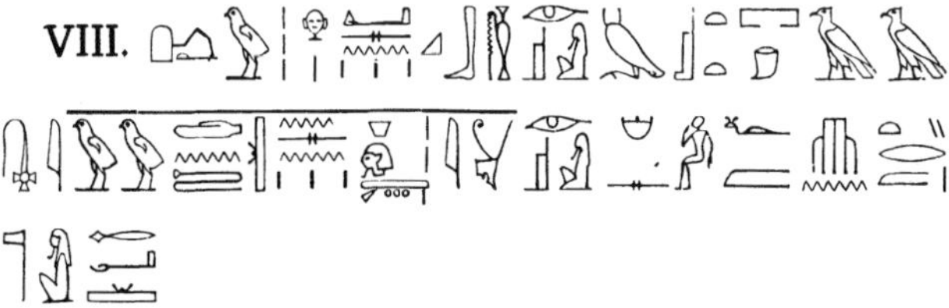

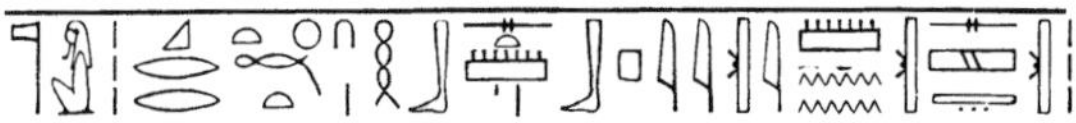

I.

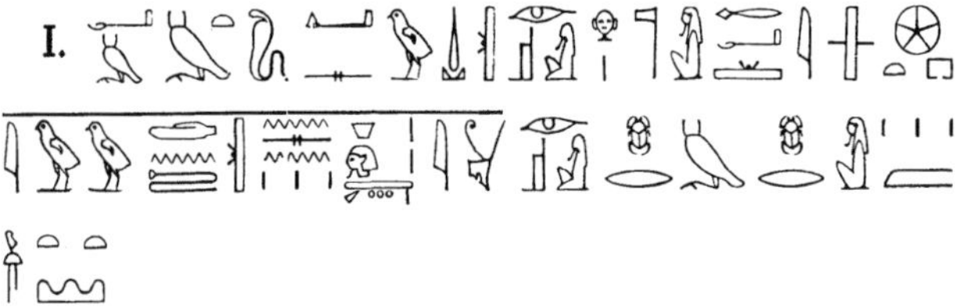

II.

III.

IV.

V.

VI.

VII.

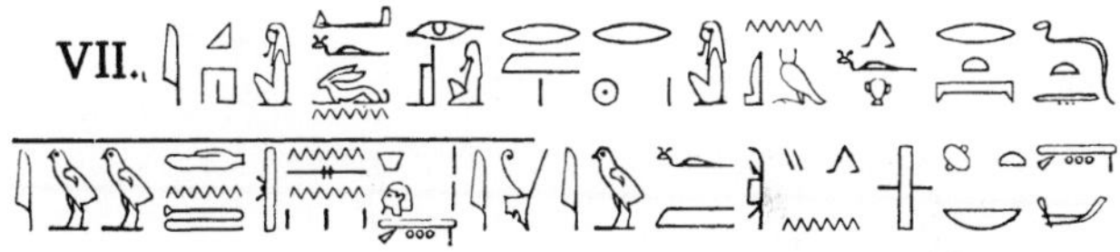

VIII.

IX.

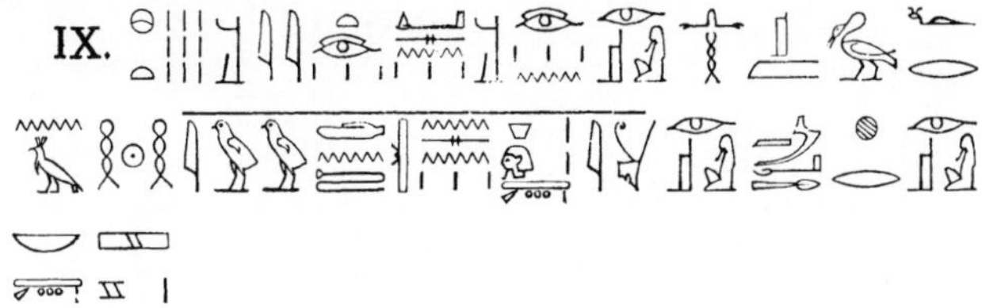

X.

XI.

XII.

XIII.

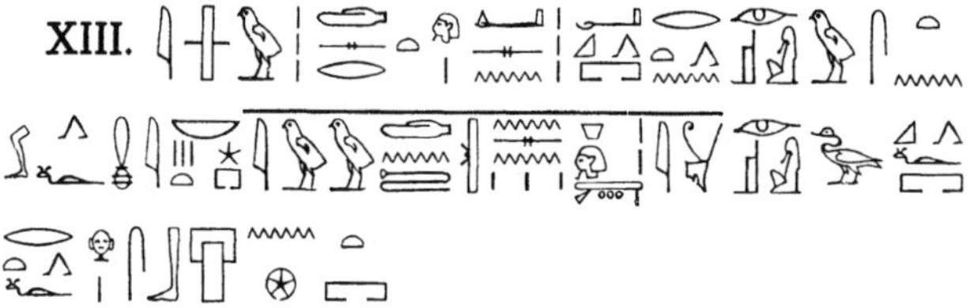

XIV.

XV.

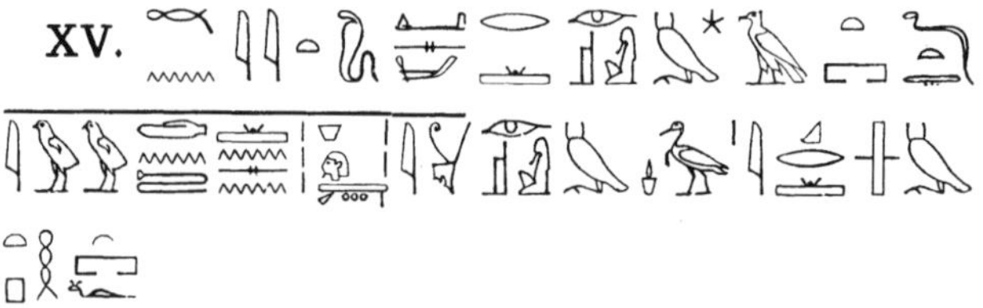

XVI.

XVII.

XVIII.

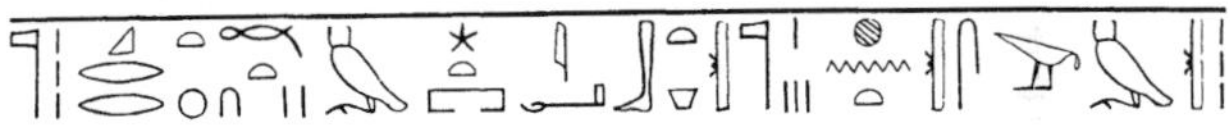

I.

II.

III.

IV.

V.

VI.

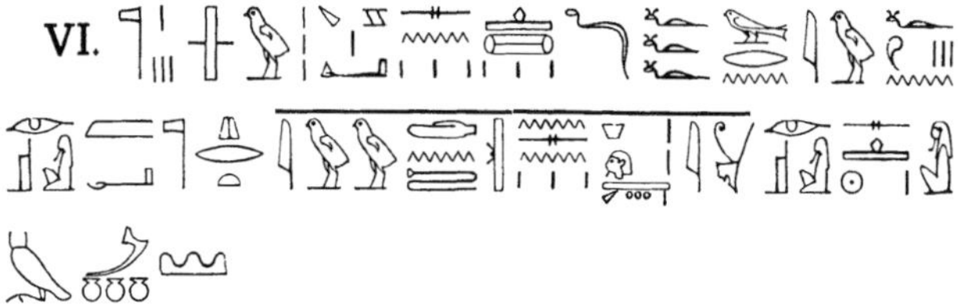

VII.

VIII.

IX.

Chapter CLXIX.

[From the Papyrus of Nefer-uben-f (Naville, *op. cit.,* Bd. I, Bl. 190).]

6
7
8
9
10
11

12
13
14
15
16
17

18
19
20
21
22
23
24

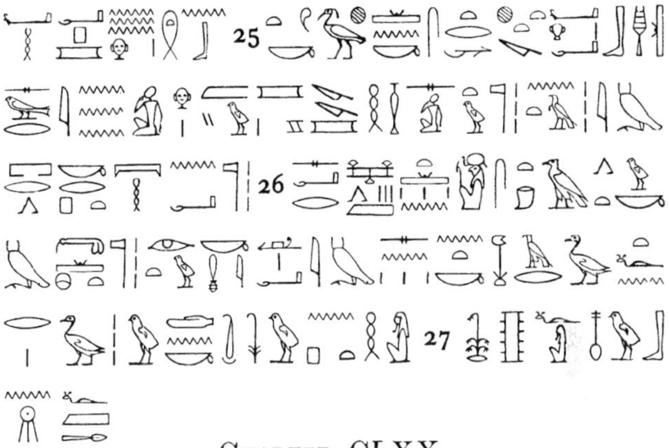

CHAPTER CLXX.

[From the Papyrus of Nefer-uben-f (Naville, *op. cit.*, Bd. I, Bl. 191).]

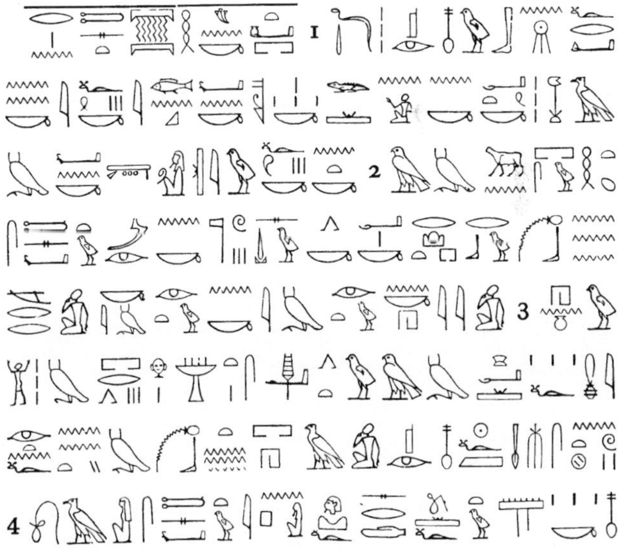

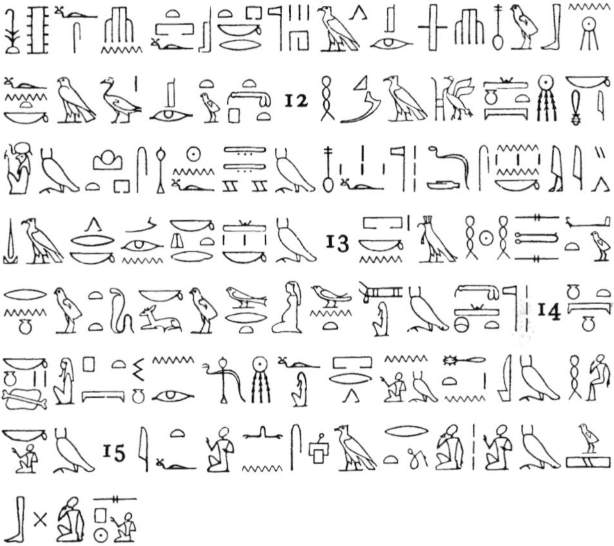

CHAPTER CLXXI.

[From the Papyrus of Ȧmen-ḥetep (Mariette, Papyrus de Boulaq, tome III, pl. 7).]

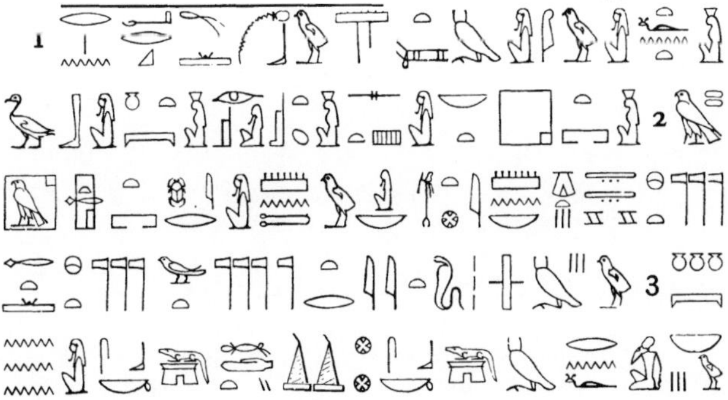

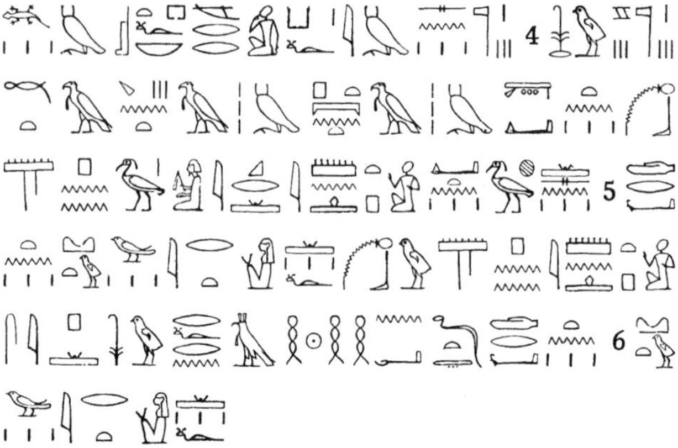

CHAPTER CLXXII.

[From the Papyrus of Nebseni (Brit. Mus. No. 9,900, sheets 32, 33).]

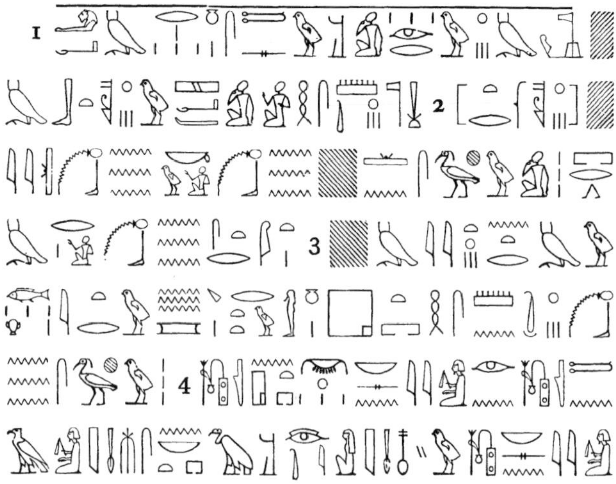

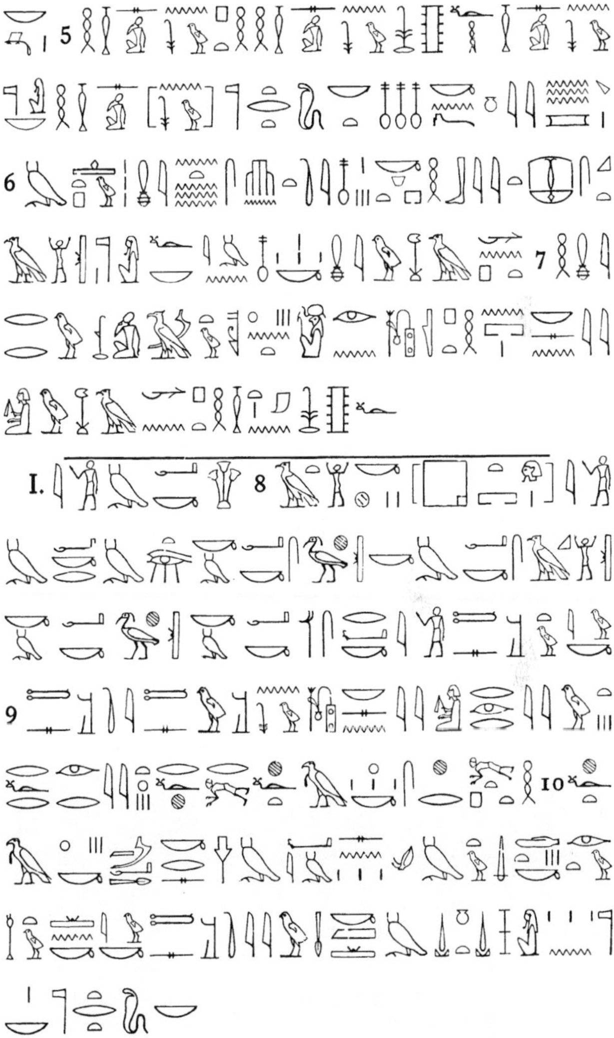

II. 11

[Hieroglyphic text, line 18]

[Hieroglyphic text]

III. [Hieroglyphic text]

[Hieroglyphic text, line 19]

[Hieroglyphic text]

[Hieroglyphic text, line 20]

[Hieroglyphic text]

[Hieroglyphic text, line 21]

[Hieroglyphic text]

[Hieroglyphic text, line 22]

[Hieroglyphic text]

IV. [Hieroglyphic text]

[Hieroglyphic text, line 23]

[Hieroglyphic text]

[Hieroglyphic text, line 24]

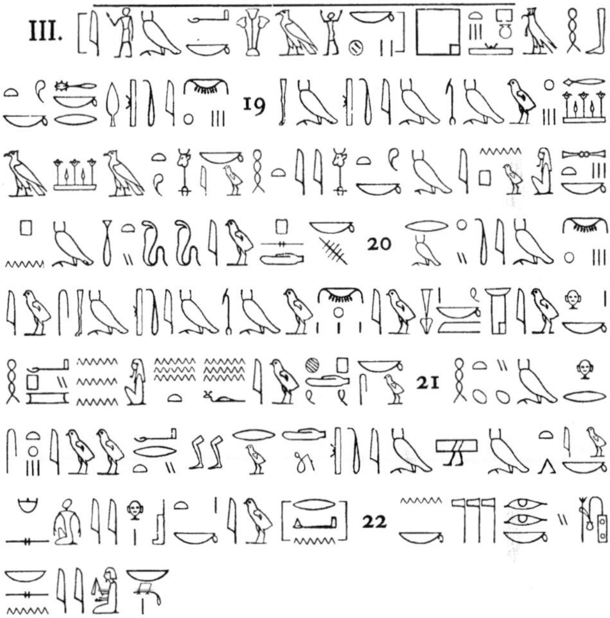

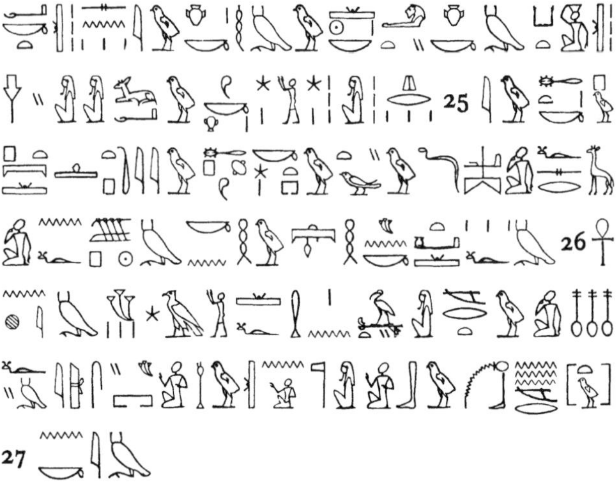

V.

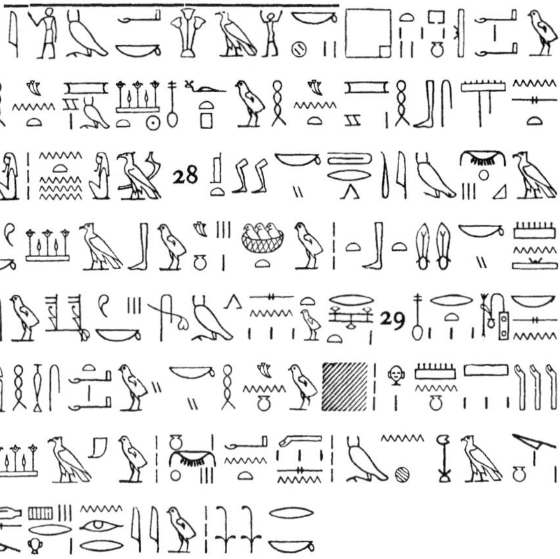

VI.

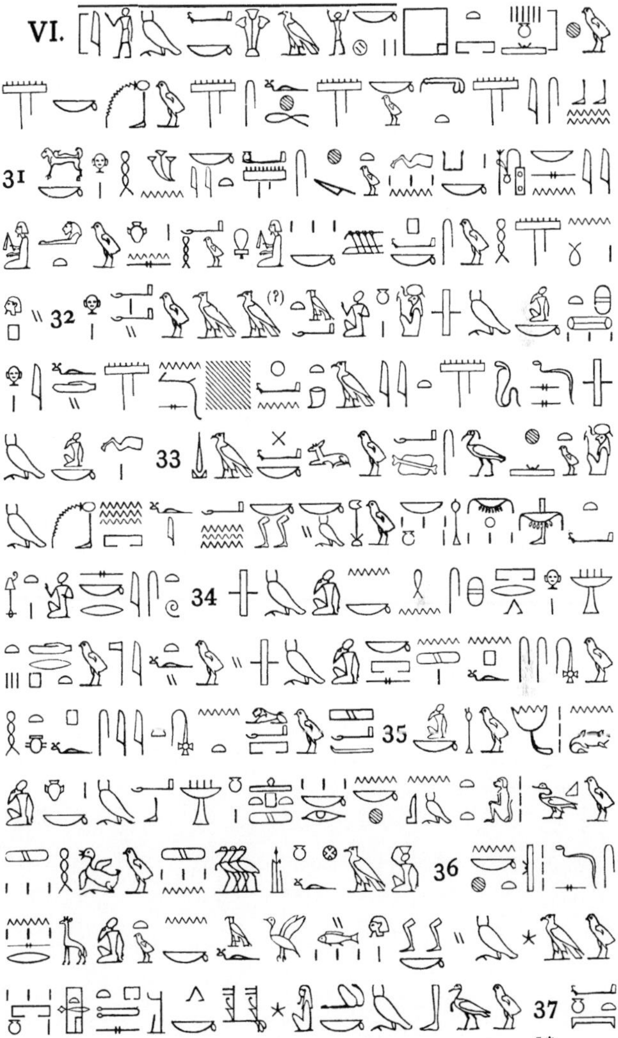

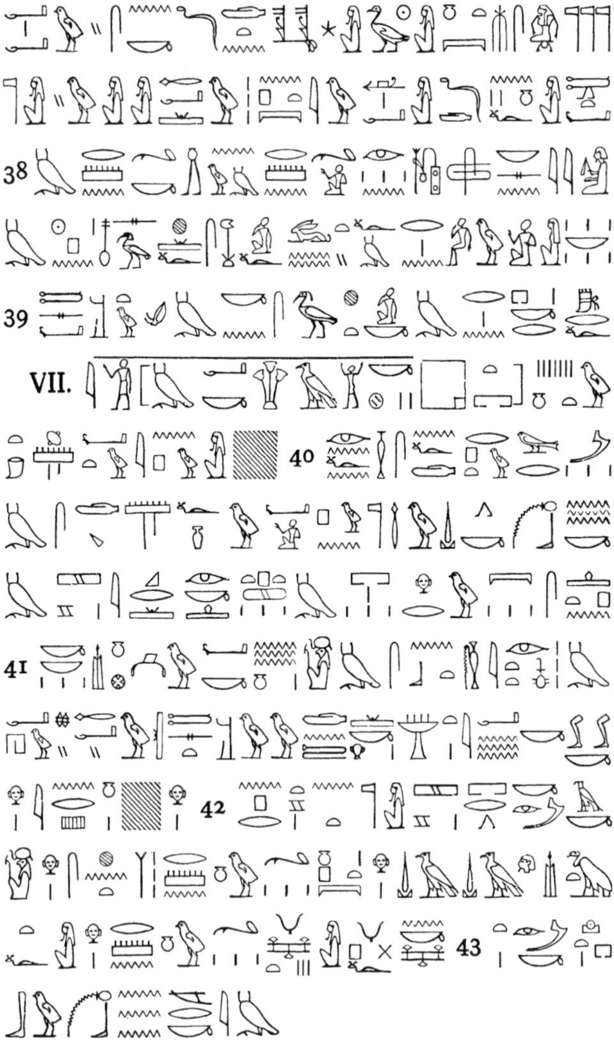
38
39
VII.
40
41
42
43

VIII. [hieroglyphic text]

[hieroglyphic text]

44 [hieroglyphic text]

[hieroglyphic text]

45 [hieroglyphic text]

[hieroglyphic text]

[hieroglyphic text] **46** [hieroglyphic text]

IX. [hieroglyphic text]

[hieroglyphic text]

[hieroglyphic text]

[hieroglyphic text]

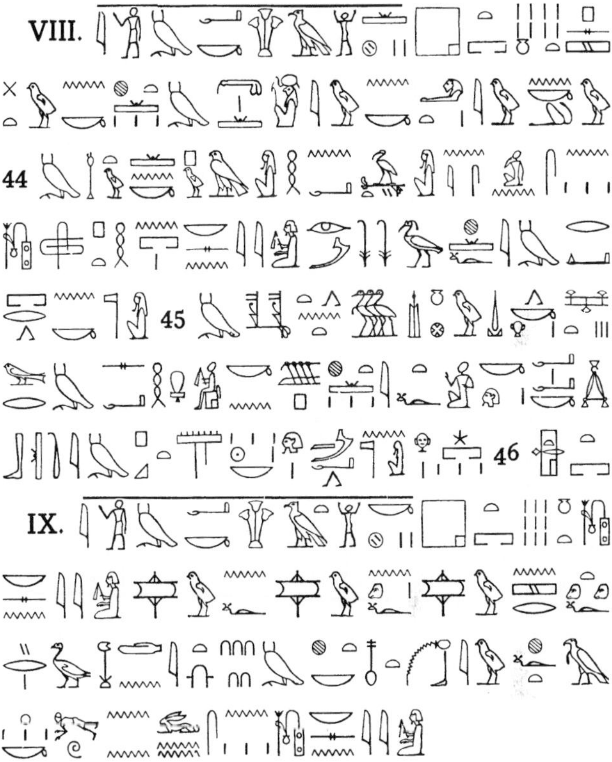

Chapter CLXXIII.

[From the Papyrus of Nebseni (Brit. Mus. No. 9,900, sheet 9).]

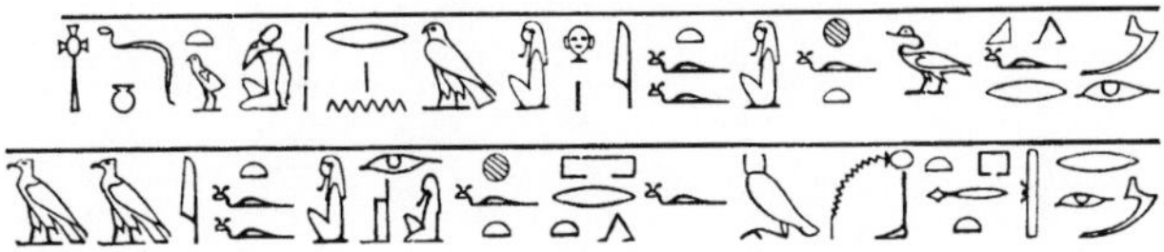

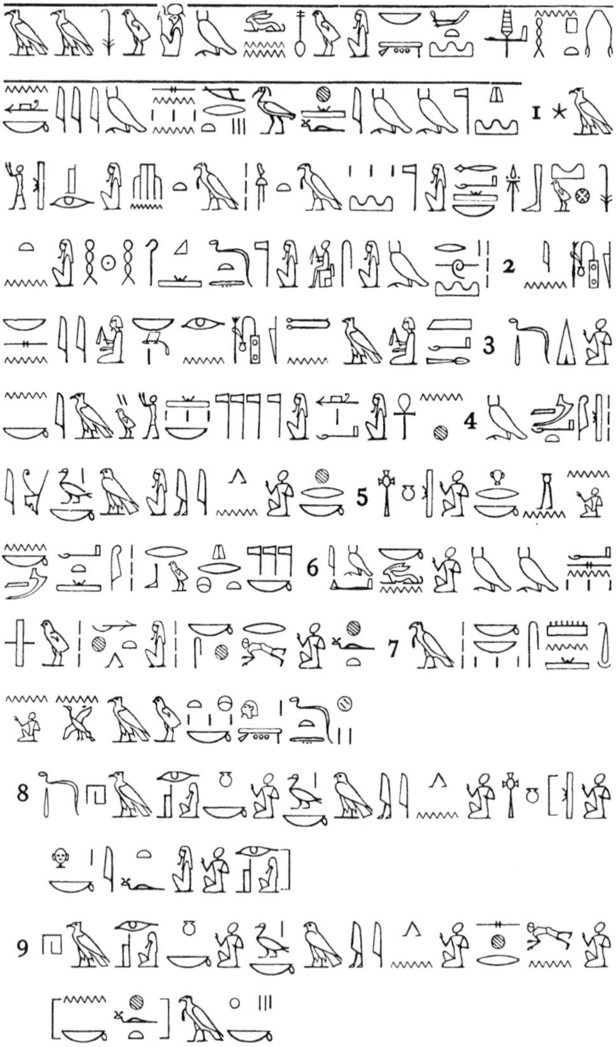

10 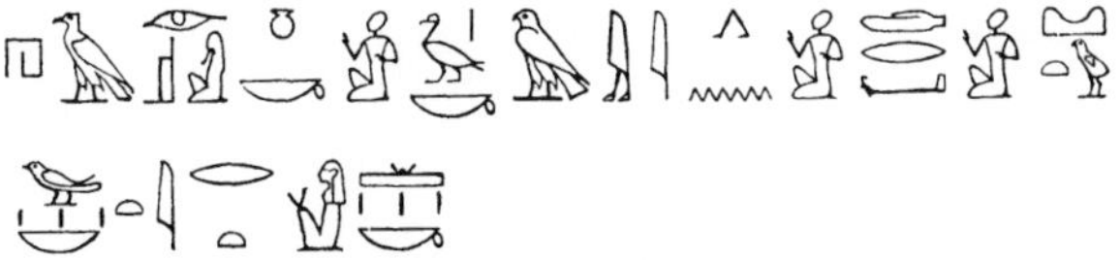

11 

12 

13 

14 

15 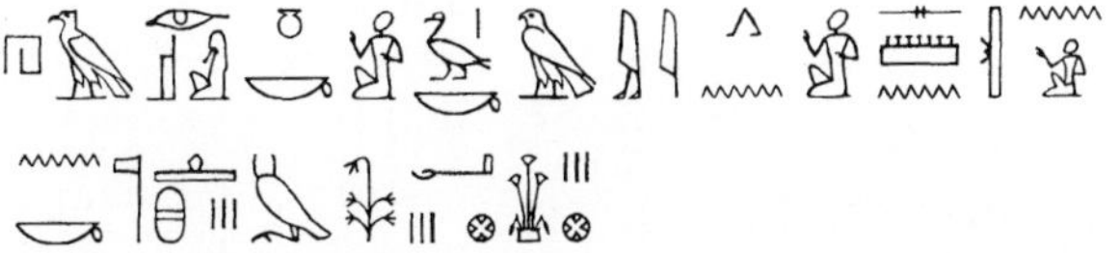

16 

17 

18 

19 

20 

21 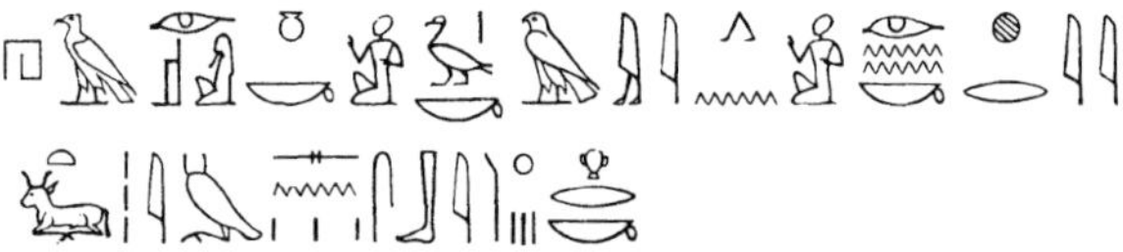

22 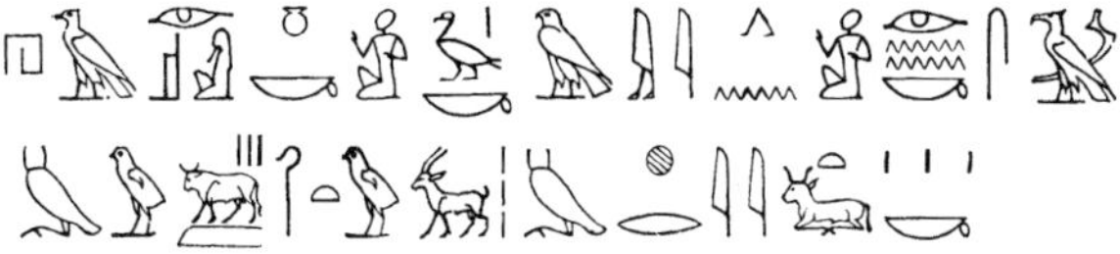

23 

24 

25 

26 

27 

28 

29 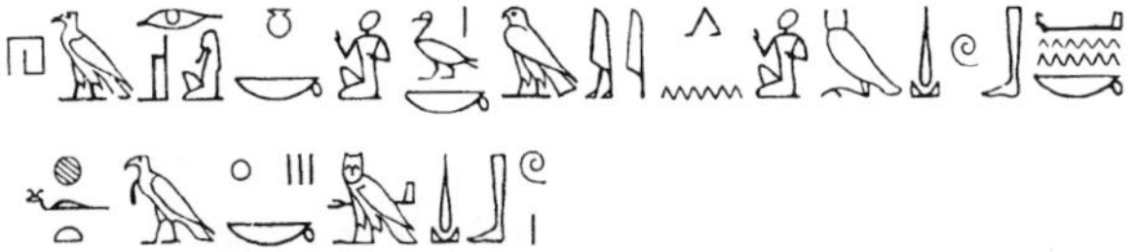

30 

31 

32 

33 

34 

35 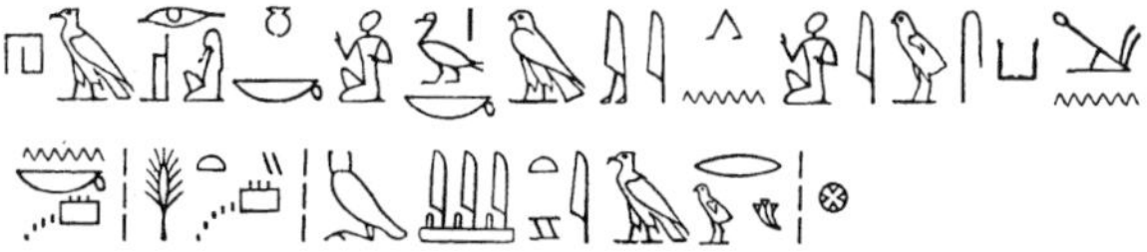

36 

37 

38 

39 

40 

41 

42 

43 

44 

45 

46 

47 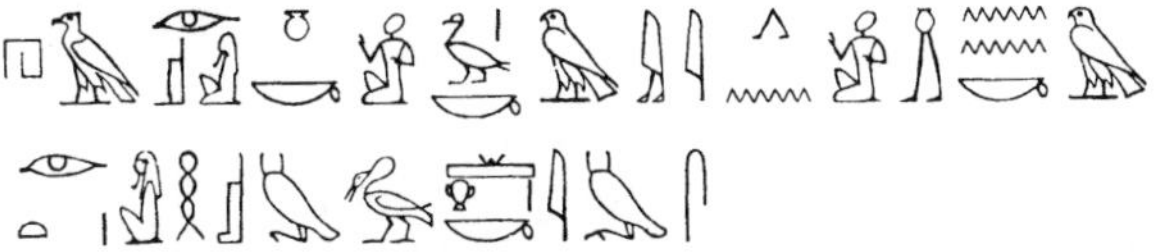

CHAPTER CLXXIV.

[From the Papyrus of Mut-ḥetep (Brit. Mus. No. 10,010, sheet 3).]

1 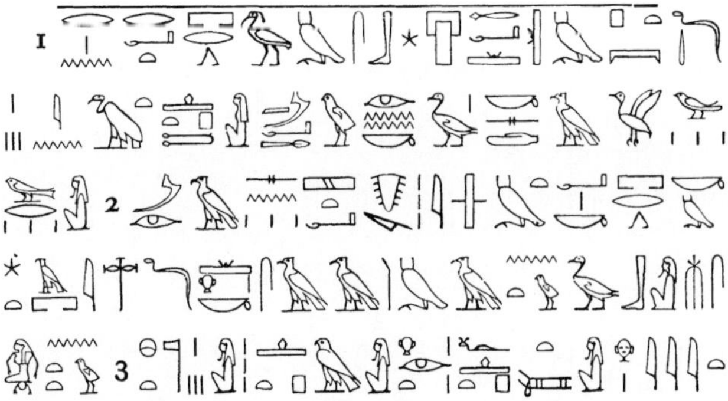

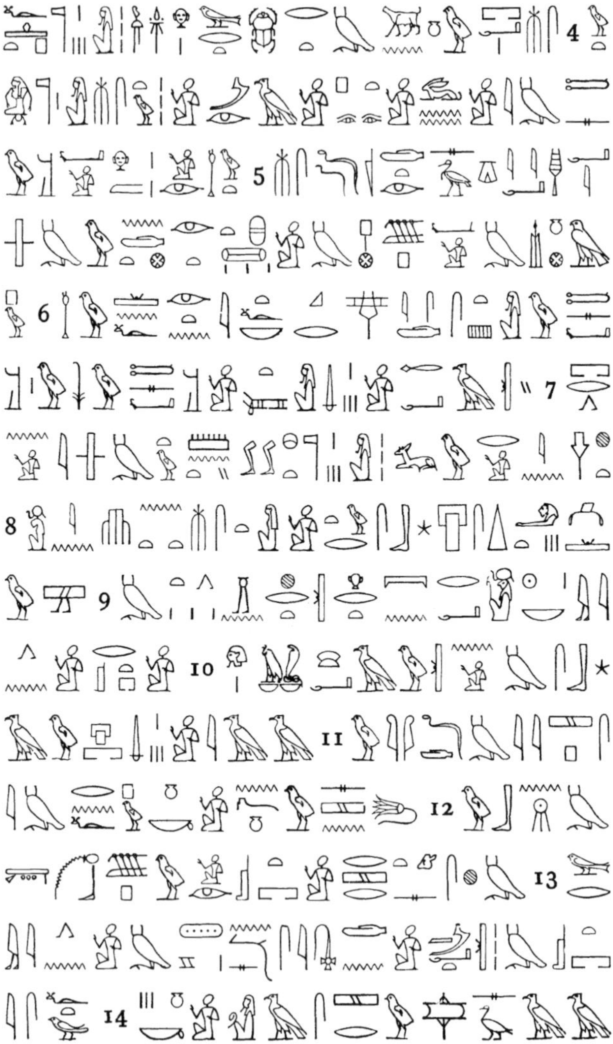

An ancient version of this Chapter is given in the Pyramid of Unȧs (see Maspero, *Recueil*, IV, p. 43, and Sethe, *Pyramidentexte*, p. 142 f). It reads:

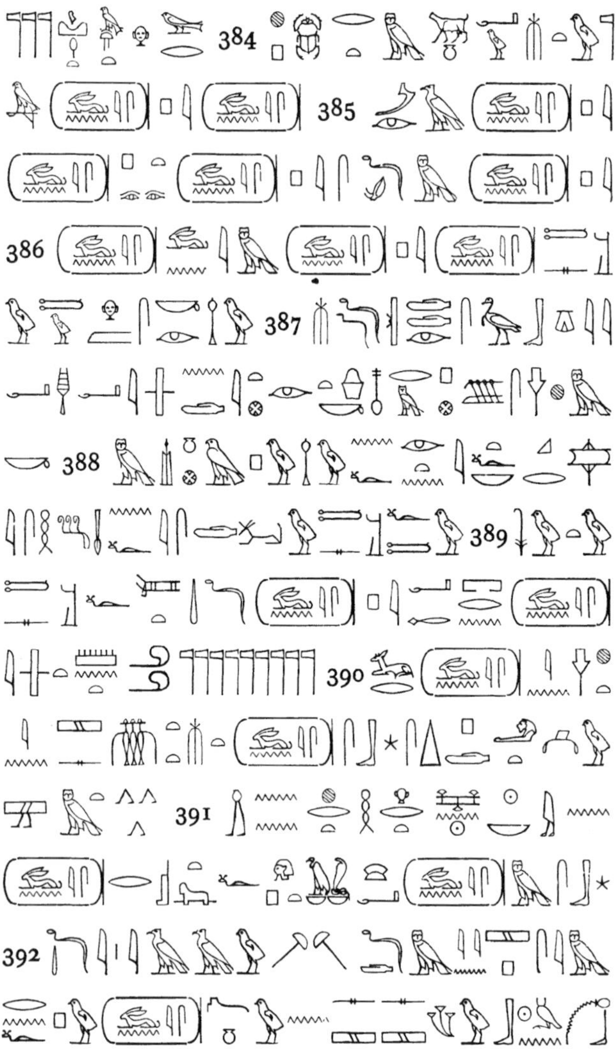
384
385
386
387
388
389
390
391
392

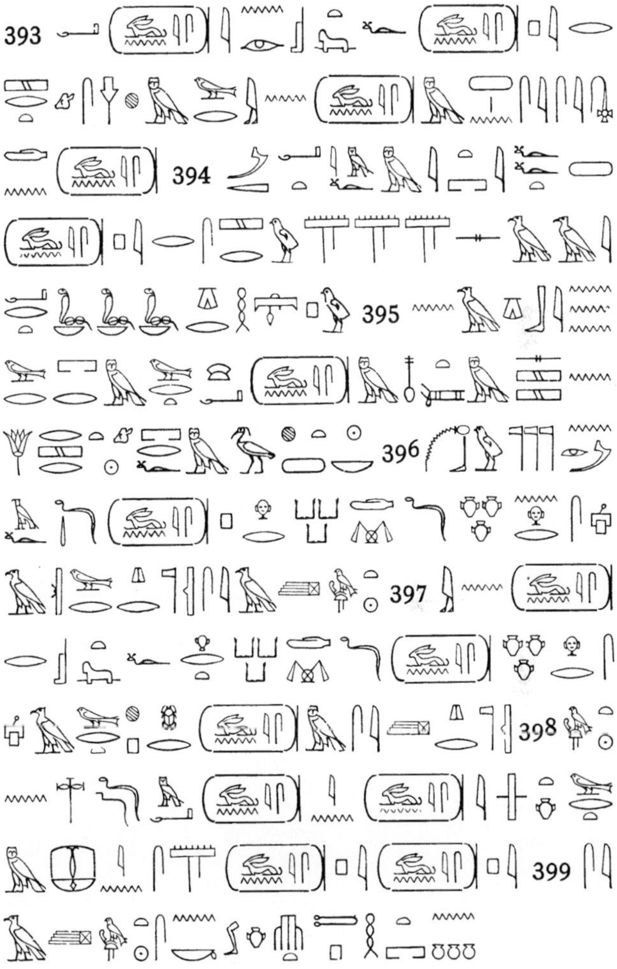
393
394
395
396
397
398
399

CHAPTER CLXXV.

[From the Papyrus of Ani (Brit. Mus. No. 10,470, sheet 29).]

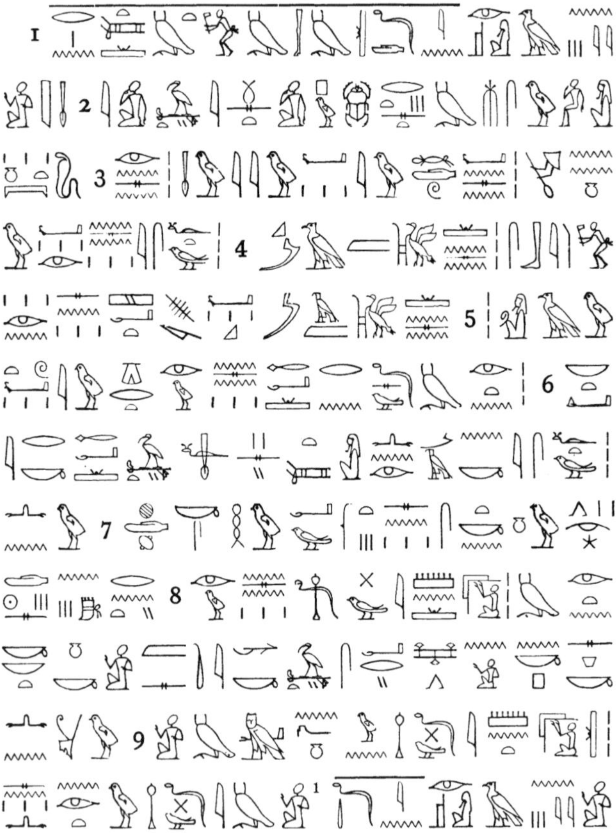

1. The Papyrus of Rā has: 

10 [hieroglyphic text]

[hieroglyphic text] 11 [hieroglyphic text]

[hieroglyphic text]

[hieroglyphic text] 12 [hieroglyphic text]

[hieroglyphic text]

[hieroglyphic text] 13 [hieroglyphic text]

[hieroglyphic text]

[hieroglyphic text] 14 [hieroglyphic text]

[hieroglyphic text] 15 [hieroglyphic text]

[hieroglyphic text]

[hieroglyphic text] 16 [hieroglyphic text]

[hieroglyphic text]

[hieroglyphic text] 9 [hieroglyphic text]

[hieroglyphic text] (Naville, *op. cit.*, I, 198).

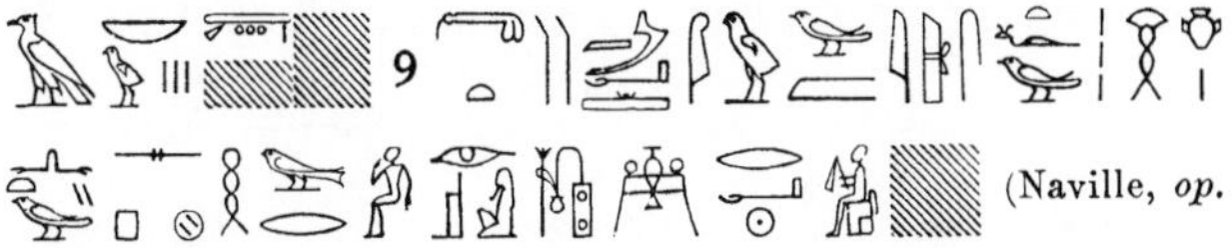

 The mutilated text of the remainder of this Chapter from the Papyrus of Rā is as follows.

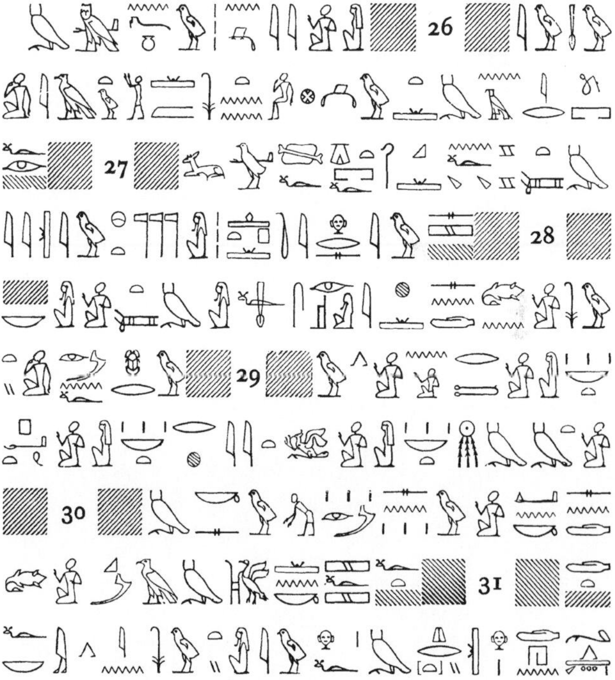

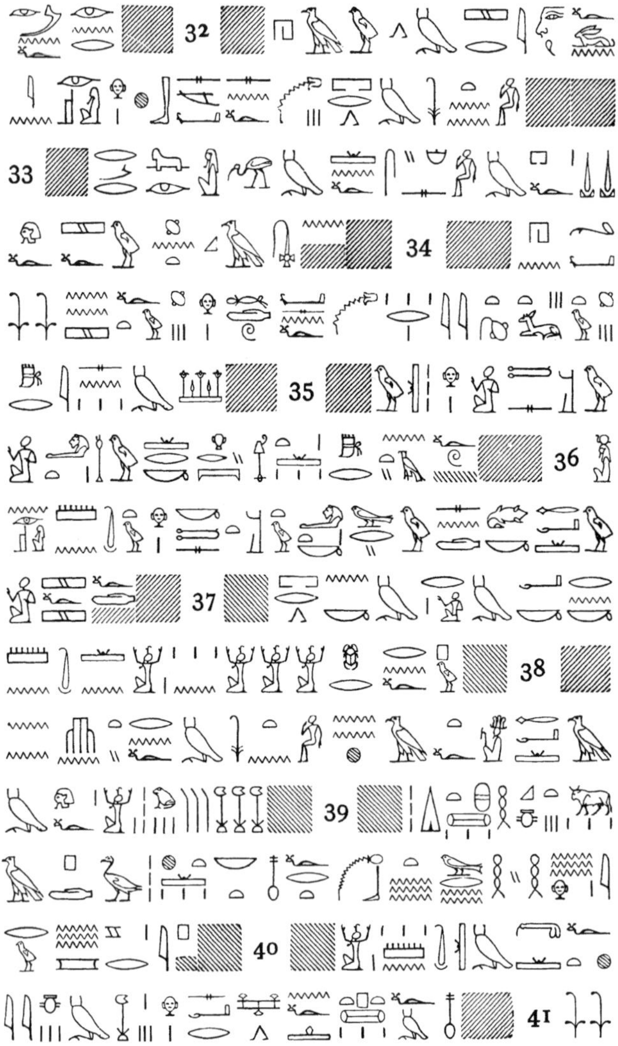
32
33
34
35
36
37
38
39
40
41

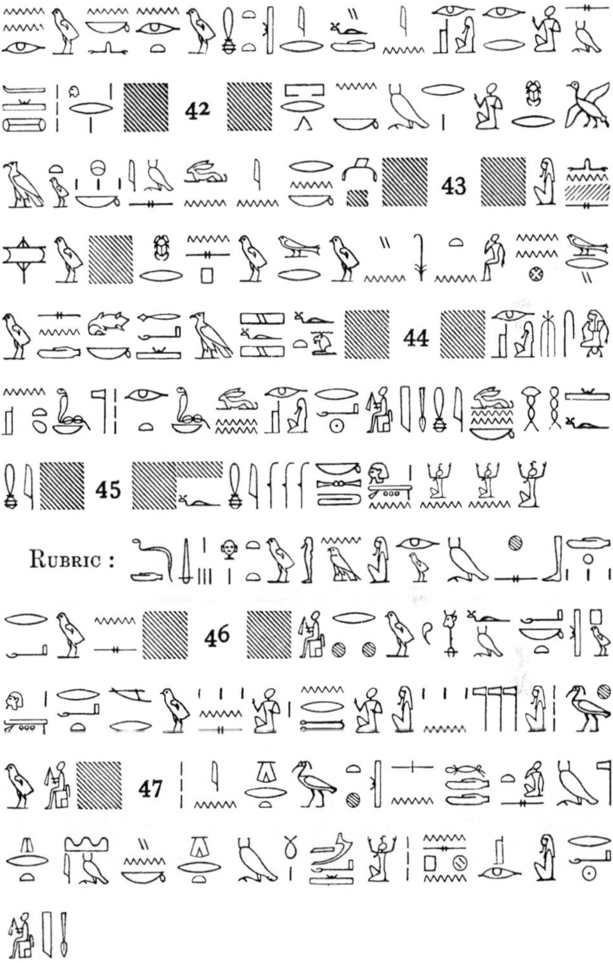
42
43
44
45
RUBRIC :
46
47

CHAPTER CLXXVI.

[From the Papyrus of Nu (Brit. Mus. No. 10,477, sheet 22).]

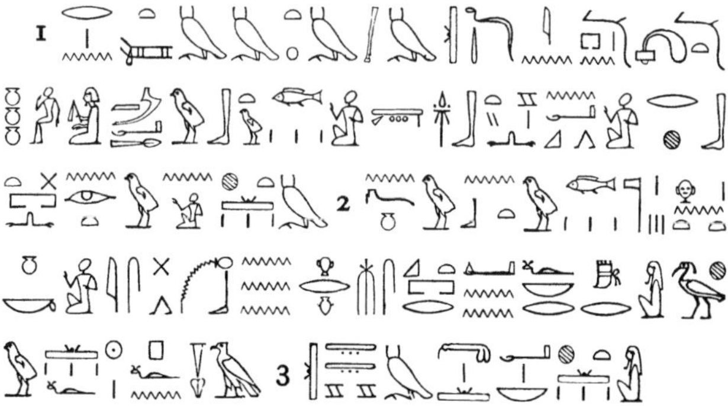

RUBRIC:

An ancient version of this Chapter is given in the Pyramid of Unȧs (see Maspero, *Recueil*, IV, p. 42 and Sethe, *Pyramidentexte*, p. 137). It reads:

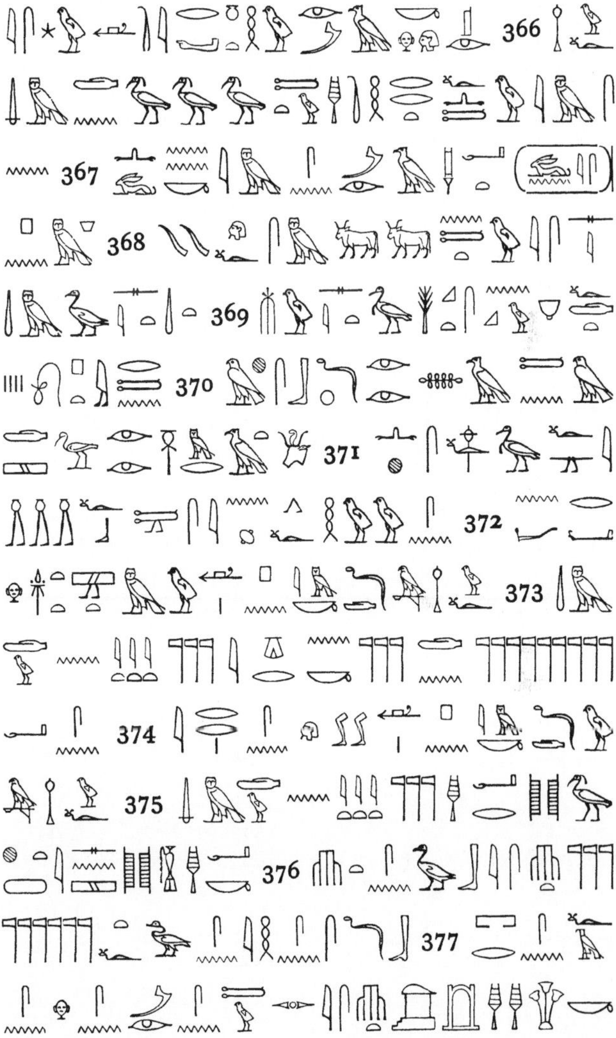
366
367
368
369
370
371
372
373
374
375
376
377

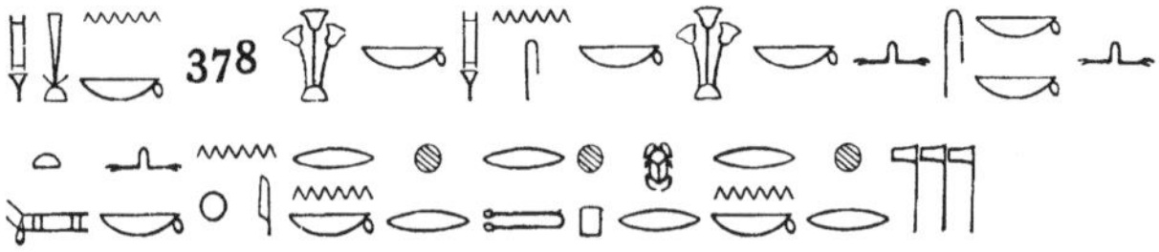

CHAPTER CLXXVII.

[From the Papyrus of Nebseni (Brit. Mus. No. 9,900, sheet 18).]

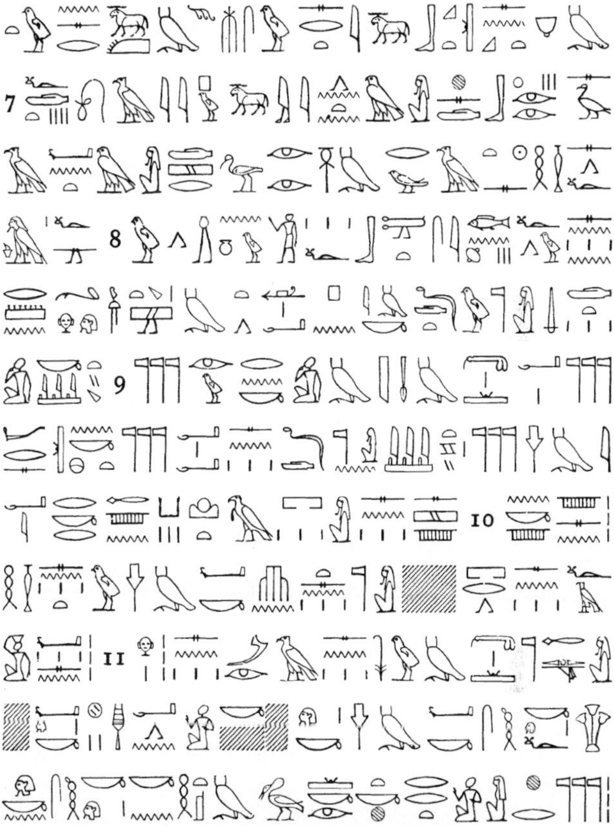

CHAPTER CLXXVIII.

[From the Papyrus of Nebseni (Brit. Mus. No. 9,900, sheet 19).]

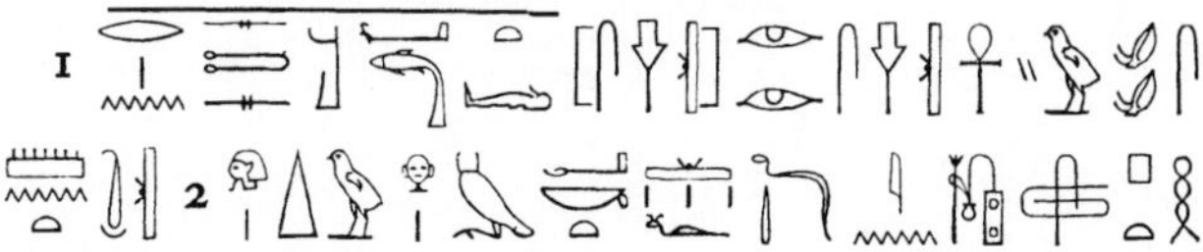

18
19
20
21
22
23
24

25

26

27

28

29

30

31

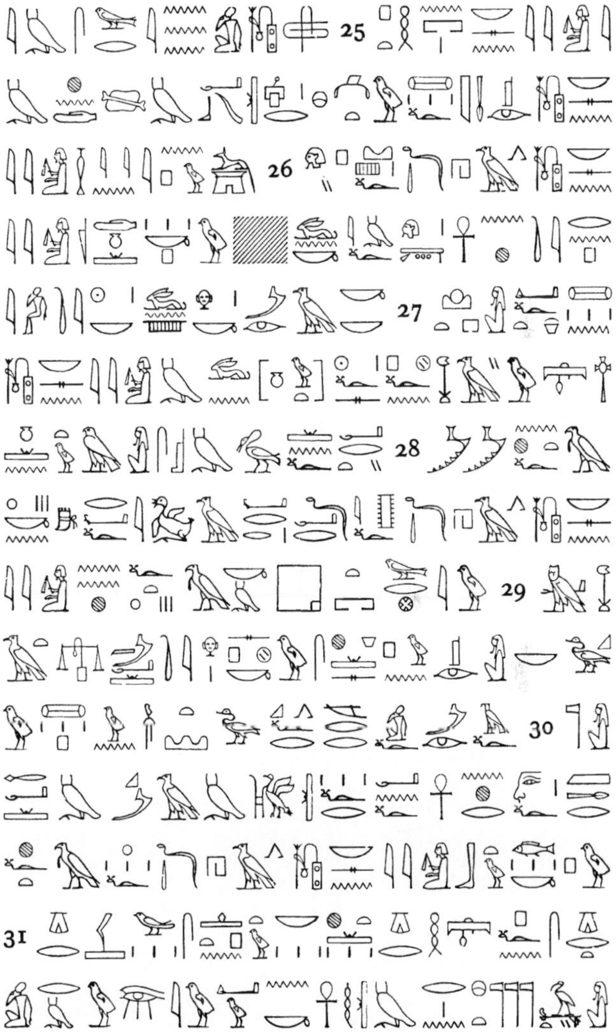

An ancient version of a portion of this Chapterr is given in the Pyramid of Unȧs (see Maspero, *Recueil*, III, p. 195, and Sethe, *Pyramidentexte*, p. 67 f.). It reads:

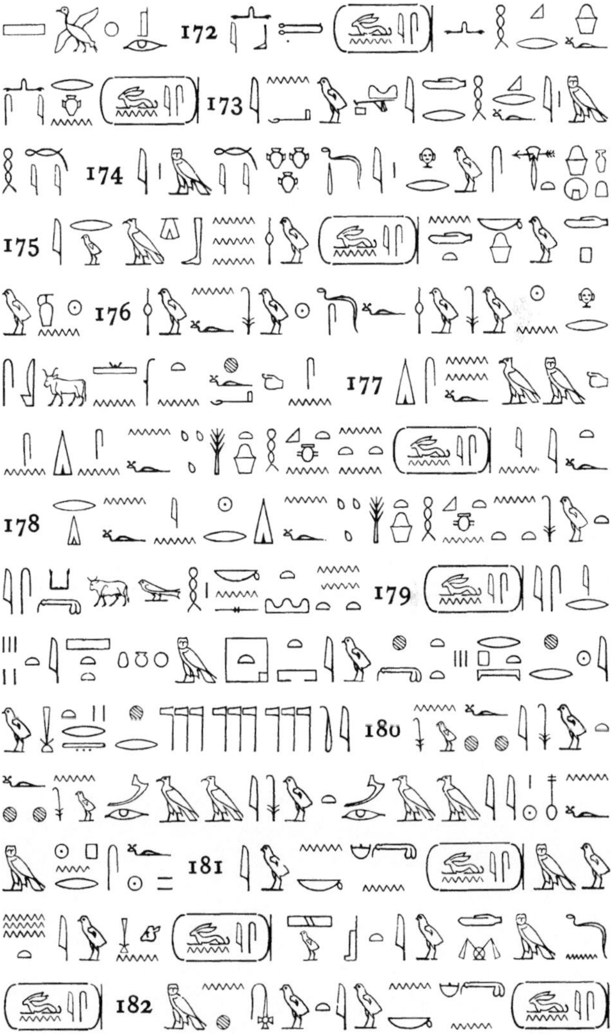
172
173
174
175
176
177
178
179
180
181
182

183
184
185
186
187
188
189

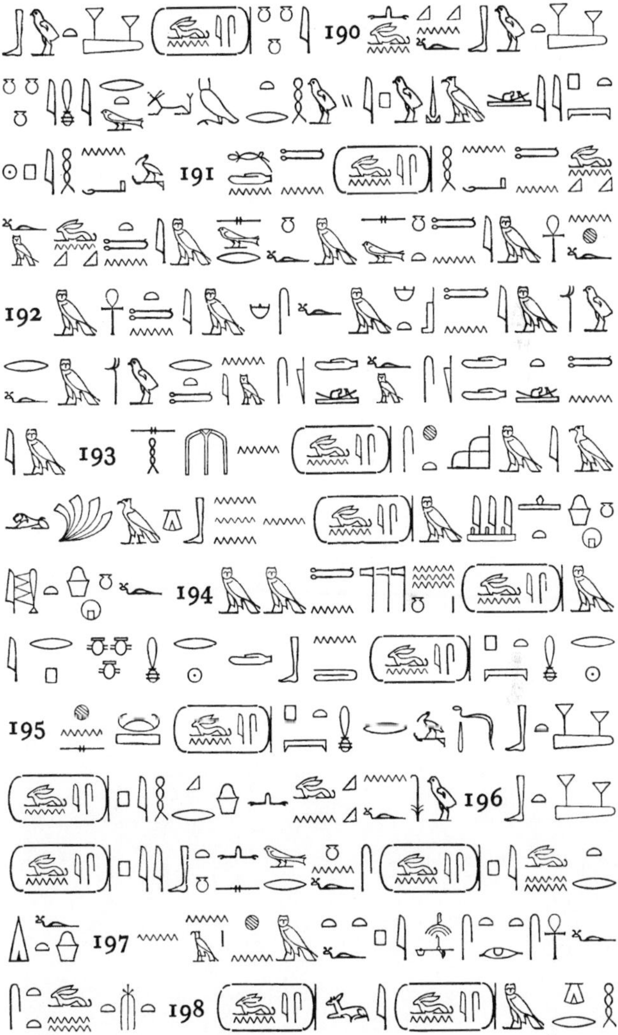
190
191
192
193
194
195
196
197
198

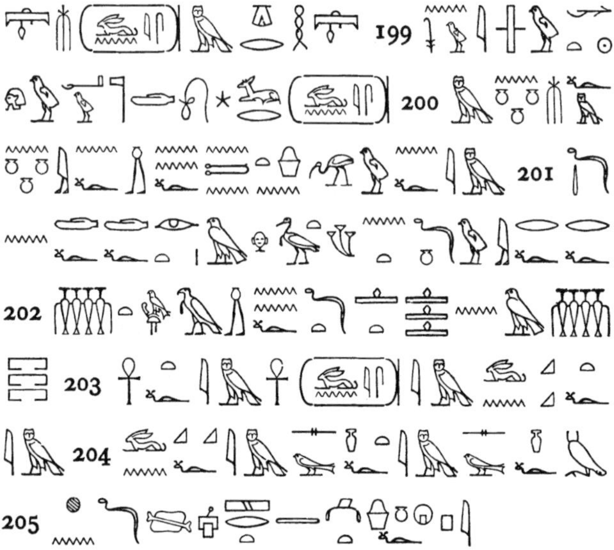

CHAPTER CLXXIX.

[From the Papyrus of Nu (Brit. Mus. No. 10,477, sheet 15).]

CHAPTER CLXXX.

[From a Papyrus at Paris (Naville, *op. cit.*, Bd. I, Bl. 204).]

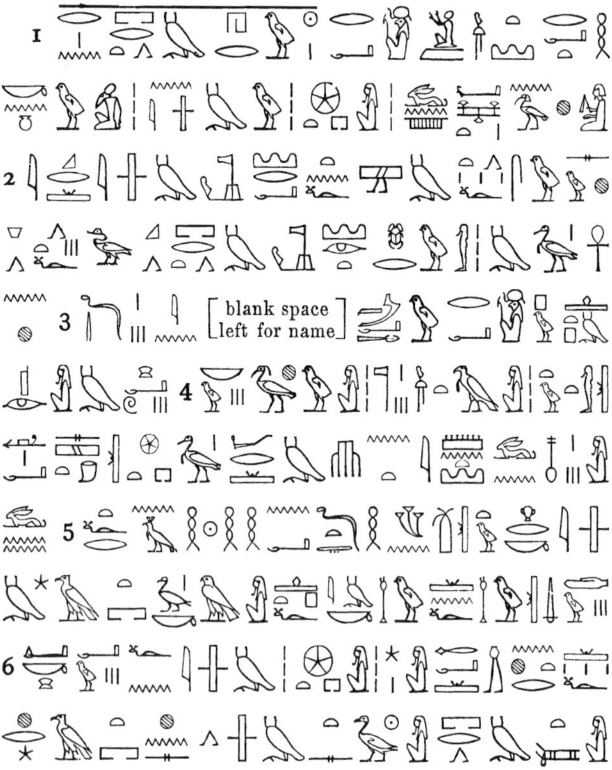

15
16
17
18
19
20
21

30
31
32
33
34
35
36
37

CHAPTER CLXXXI.

[From the Papyrus of Qenna (see Leemans, *Papyrus Égyptien*, T. 2, pl. 16).]

The following is from the Papyrus of Ȧmen-em-ȧpt, the son of Ȧbi, at Rome (see Naville, *op. cit.*, Bd. I, Bl. 206).

6
7
8
9
10
11
12

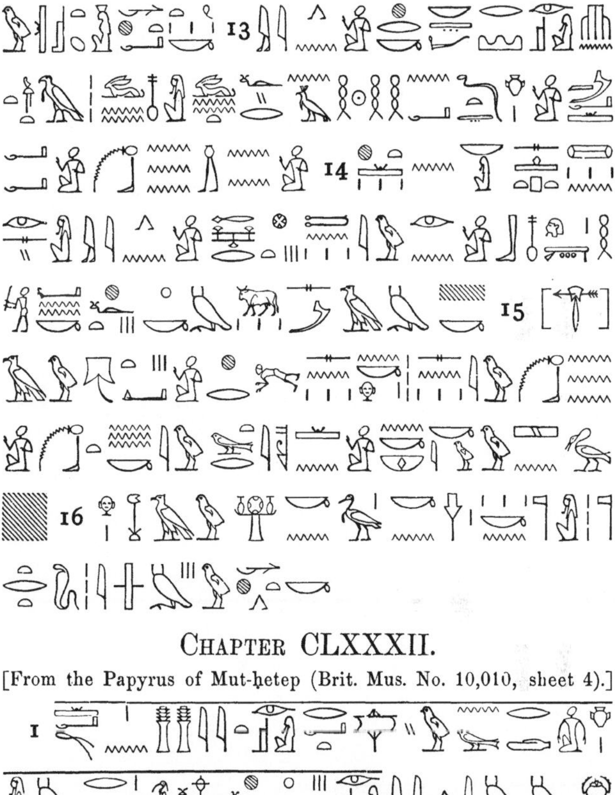

CHAPTER CLXXXII.

[From the Papyrus of Mut-ḥetep (Brit. Mus. No. 10,010, sheet 4).]

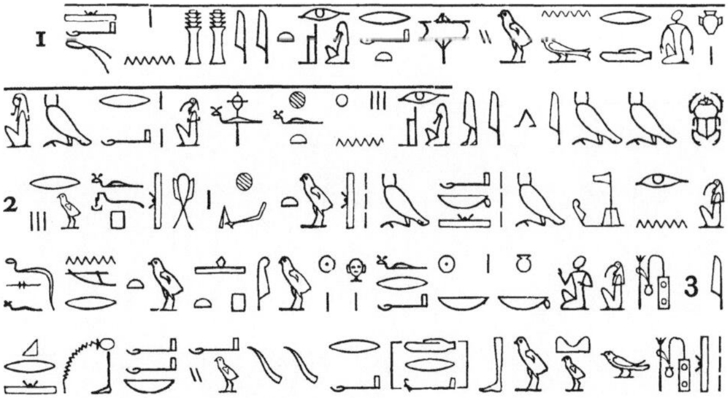

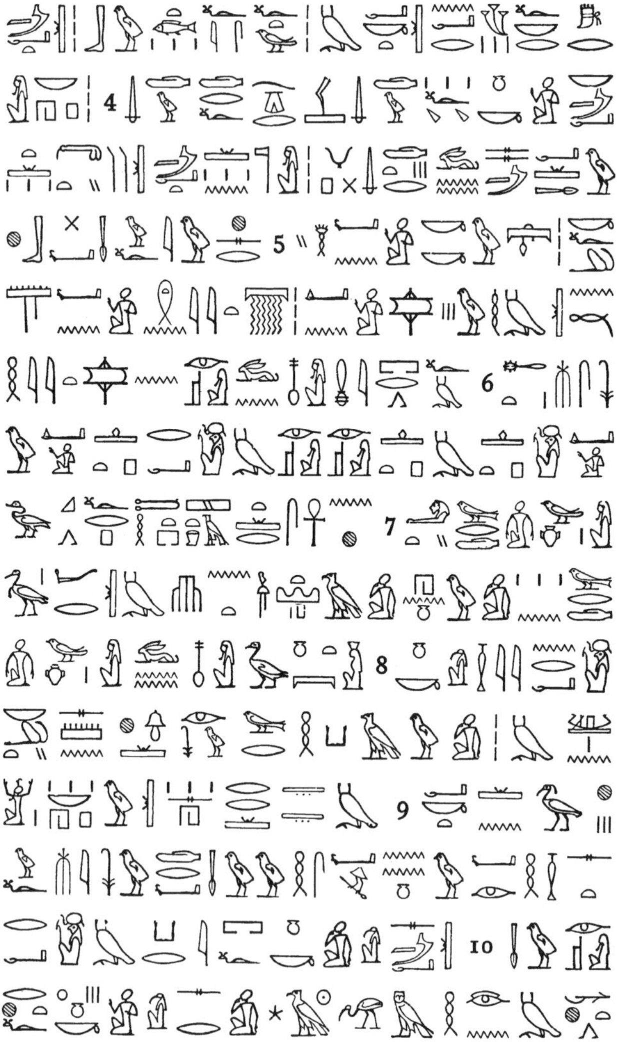

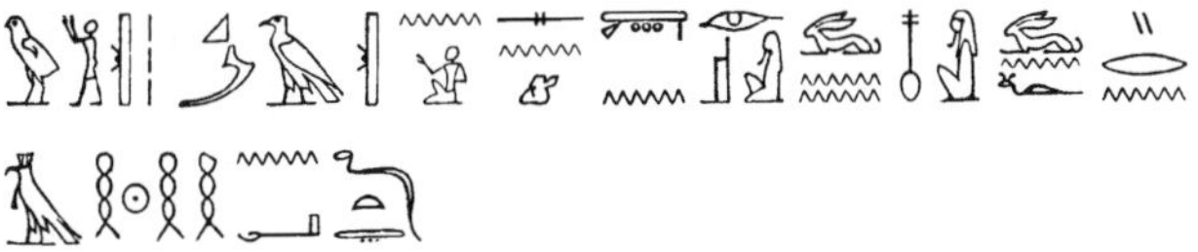

CHAPTER CLXXXIII.

[From the Papyrus of Hunefer (Brit. Mus. No. 9,901, sheet 3).]

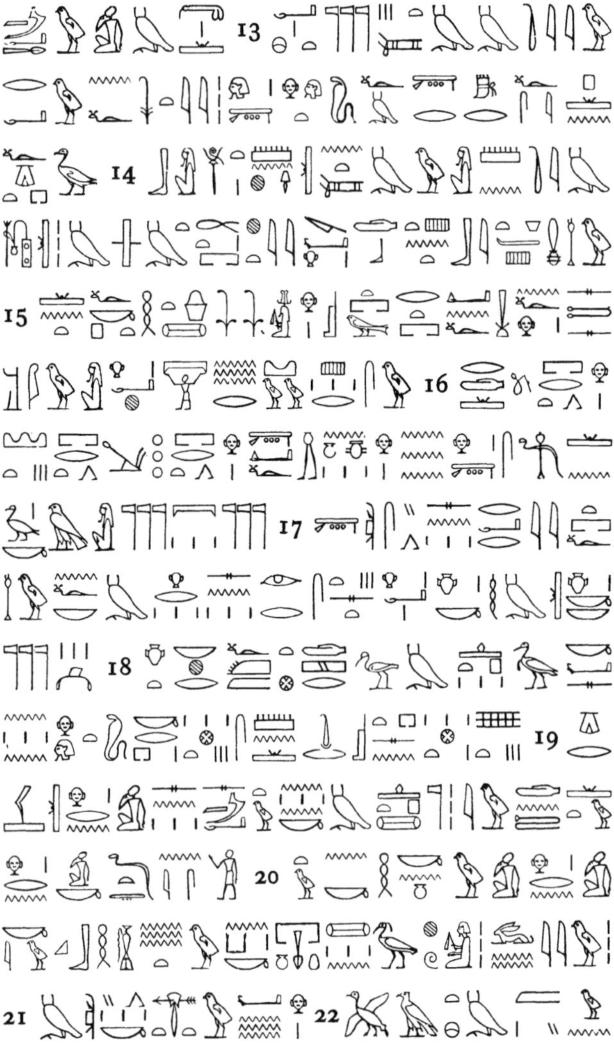

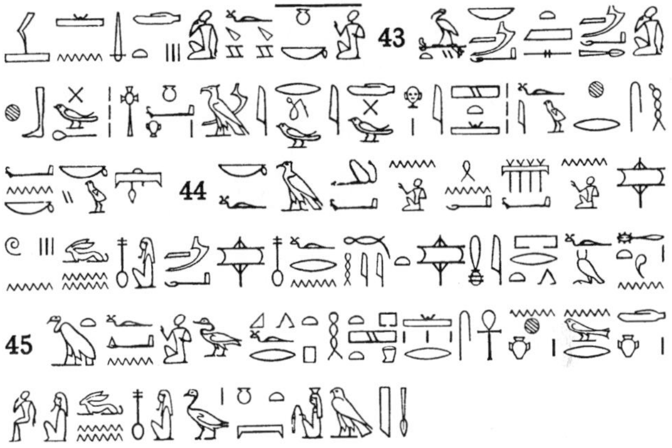

CHAPTER CLXXXIV.

[Text wanting.]

CHAPTER CLXXXV.

[From the Papyrus of Sutimes (ed. Guieyesse and Lefébure, Paris, 1877, Plate 1).]

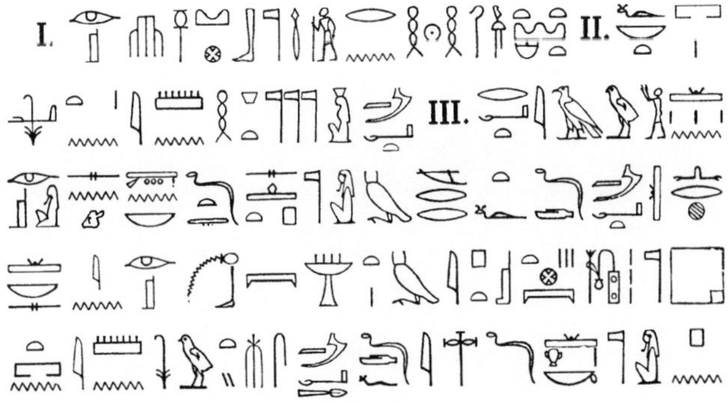

CHAPTER CLXXXVI.

[From the Papyrus of Ani (Brit. Mus. No. 10,470, sheet 37).]

CHAPTER CLXXXVII.

[From the Papyrus of Nu (Brit. Mus. No. 10,477, sheet 19).]

CHAPTER CLXXXVIII.

[From the Papyrus of Nu (Brit. Mus. No. 10,477, sheet 19).]

CHAPTER CLXXXIX.

See Vol. I, p. 160, Chapter LII B.

CHAPTER CXC. [CXLVIII.]

[From the Papyrus of Nu (Brit. Mus. No. 10,477, sheet 16).]

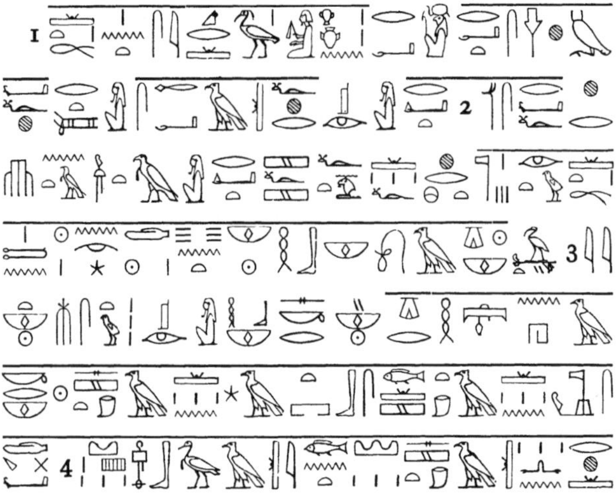

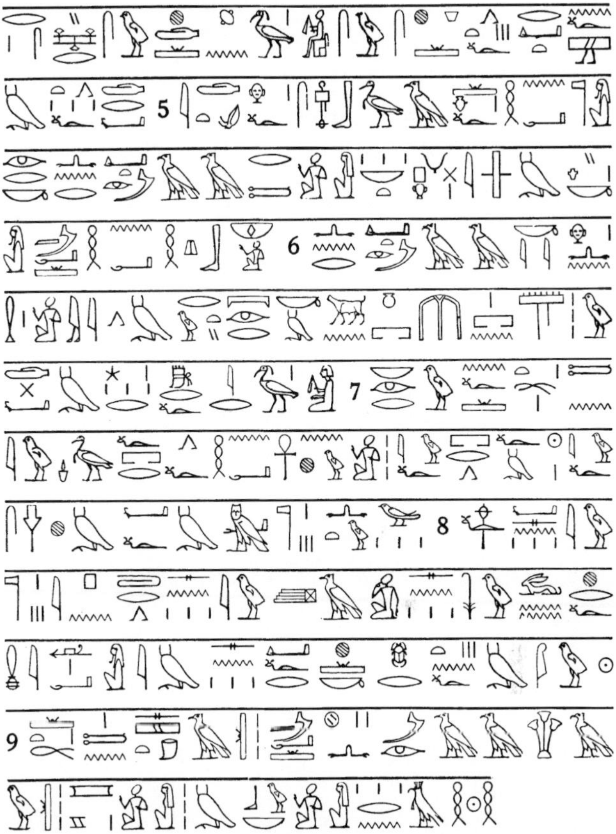

APPENDIX

I.

A Prayer for the Preservation of a Pyramid Tomb.

[Maspero, *Pyramides de Saqqarah*, p. 380.]

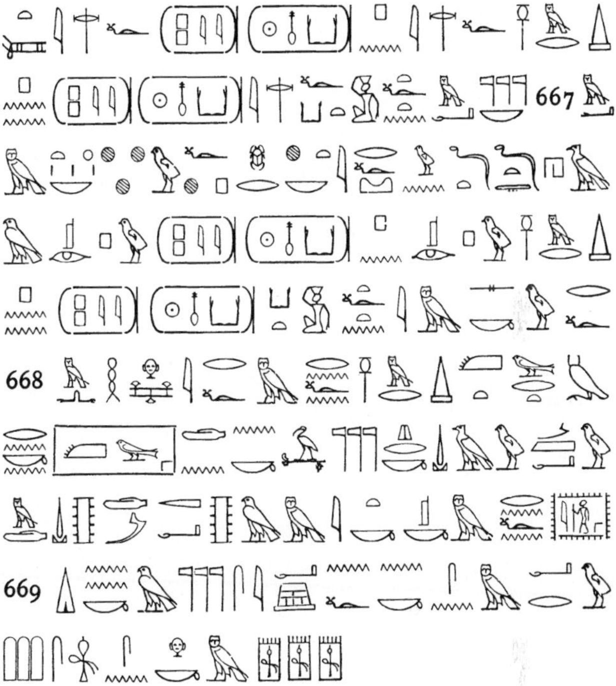

II.

The Contract between Ȧmen-Rā and Nesi-Khensu.

[Maspero, *Mémoires de la Mission*, I, p. 594 ff.]

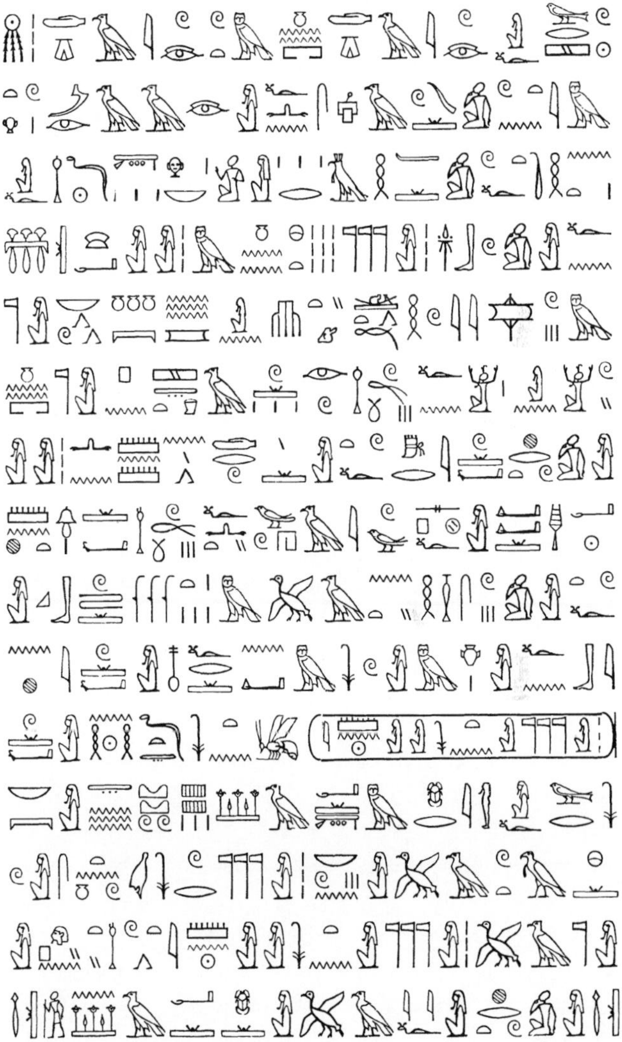

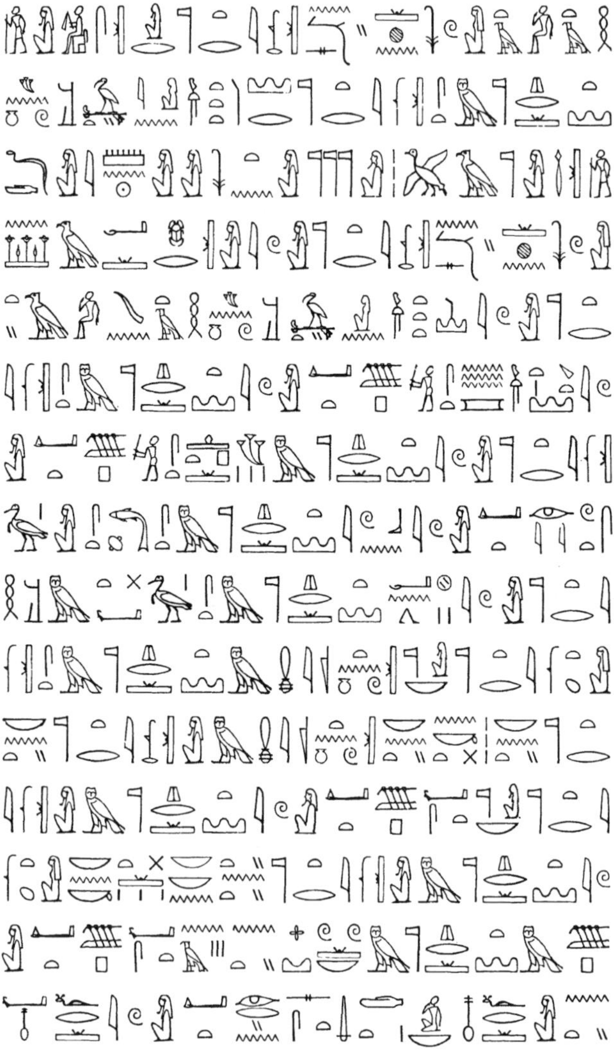

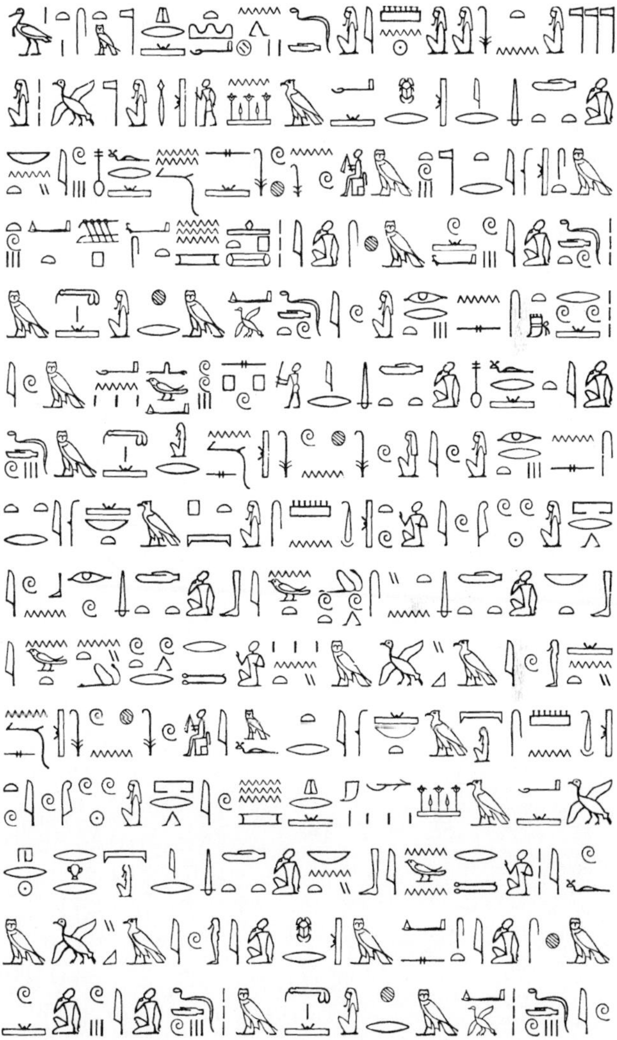

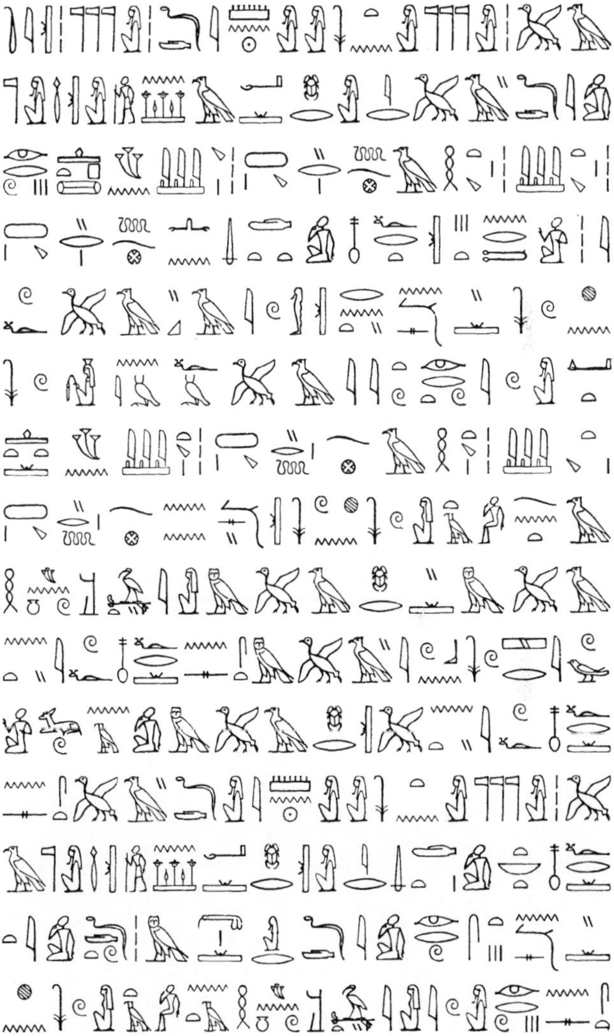

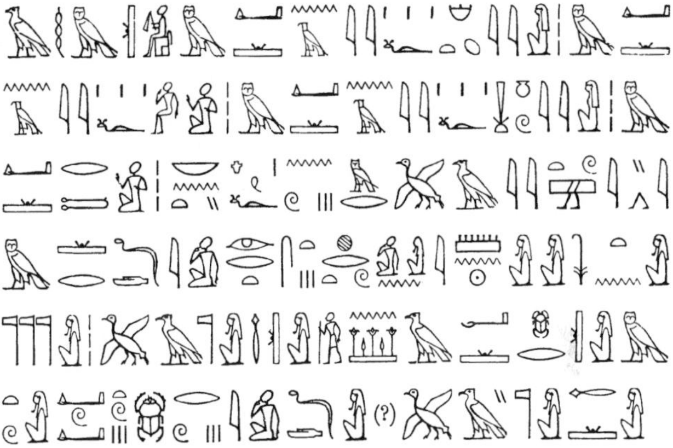

The Book of Breathings.

Part I.

[From the Papyrus of Ḳersher (Brit. Mus. No. 9,995).]

I. 1

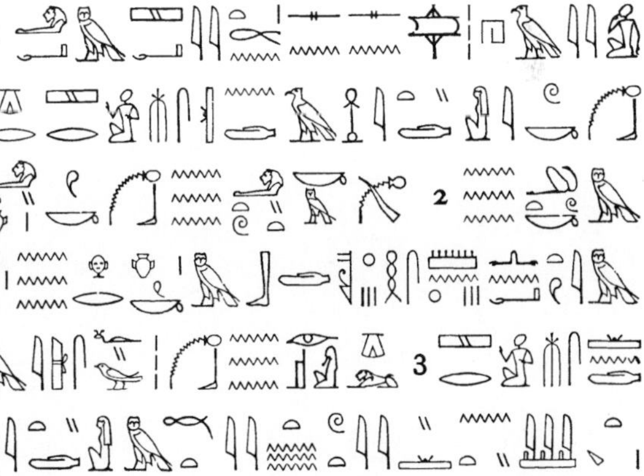

12
13
14
15
16
17
18

19
20
21
22
23
24
II. 1
2

11
12
13
14
15
16
17
18

19
20
21
22
23
24
25
III. 1

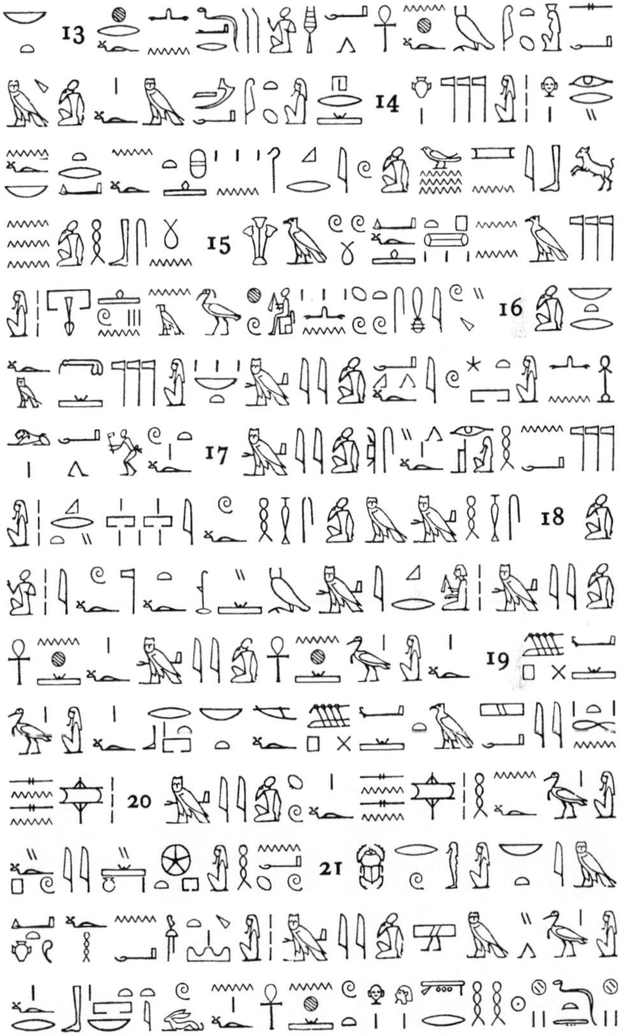
13
14
15
16
17
18
19
20
21

PART II.

[Pellegrini, *Il Libro secondo della Respirazione*, Rome, 1904.]

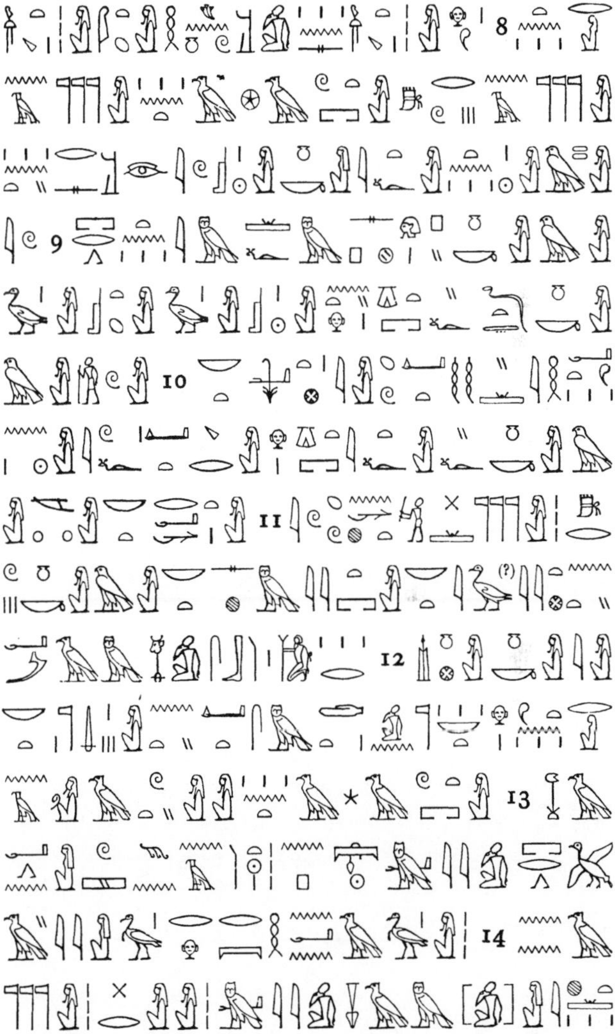

15
II. 1
2
3
4
5
6
7

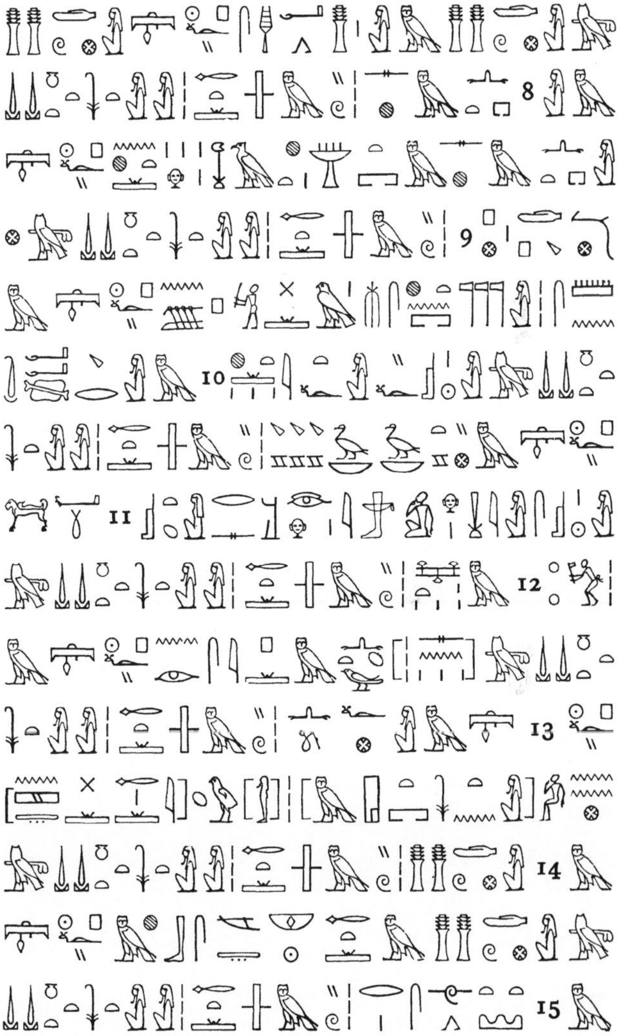

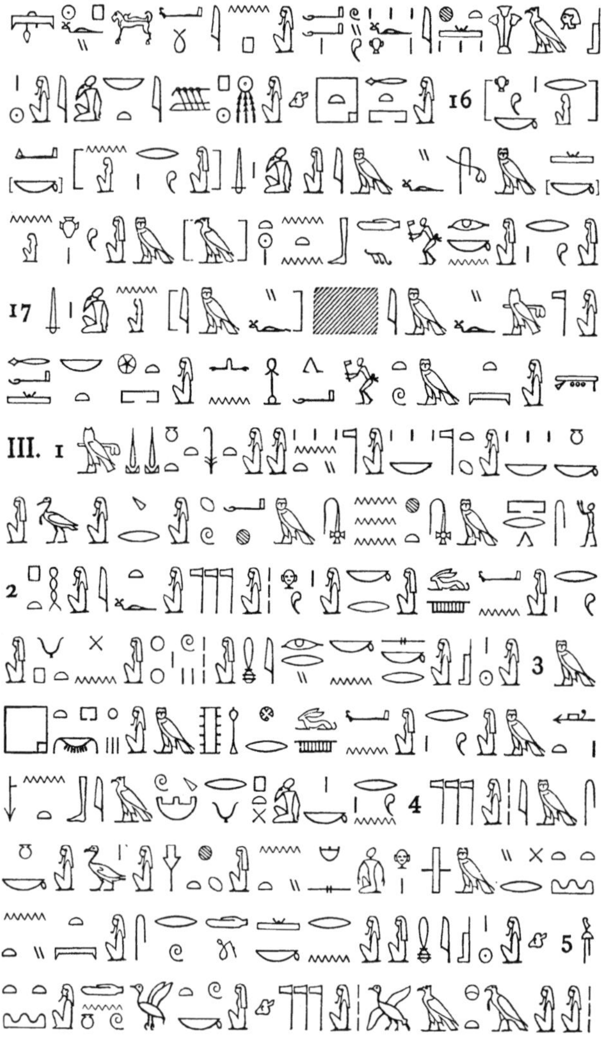
16
17
III. 1
2
3
4
5

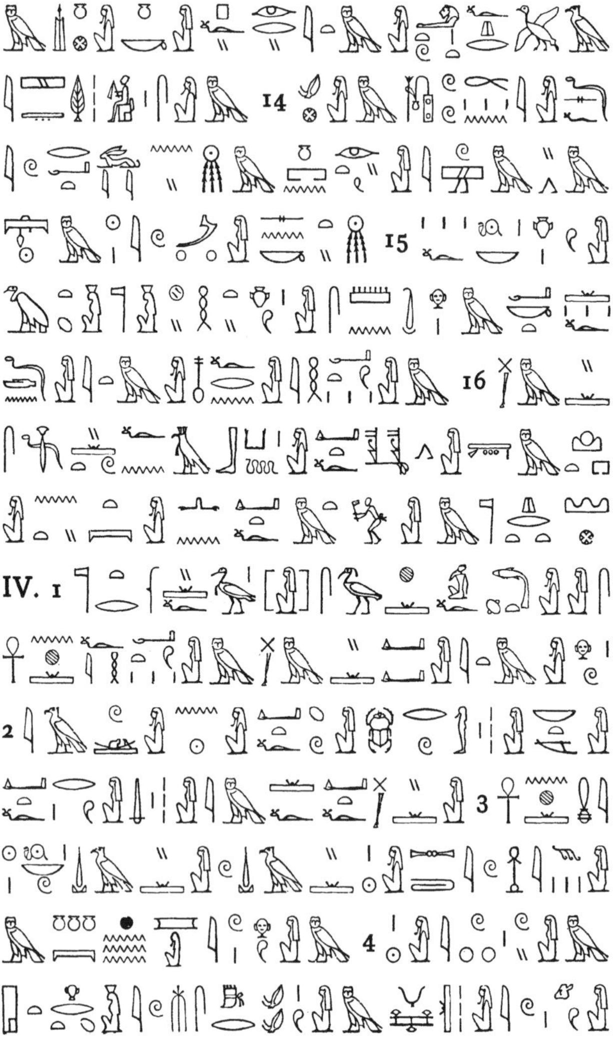
14
15
16
IV. 1
2
3
4

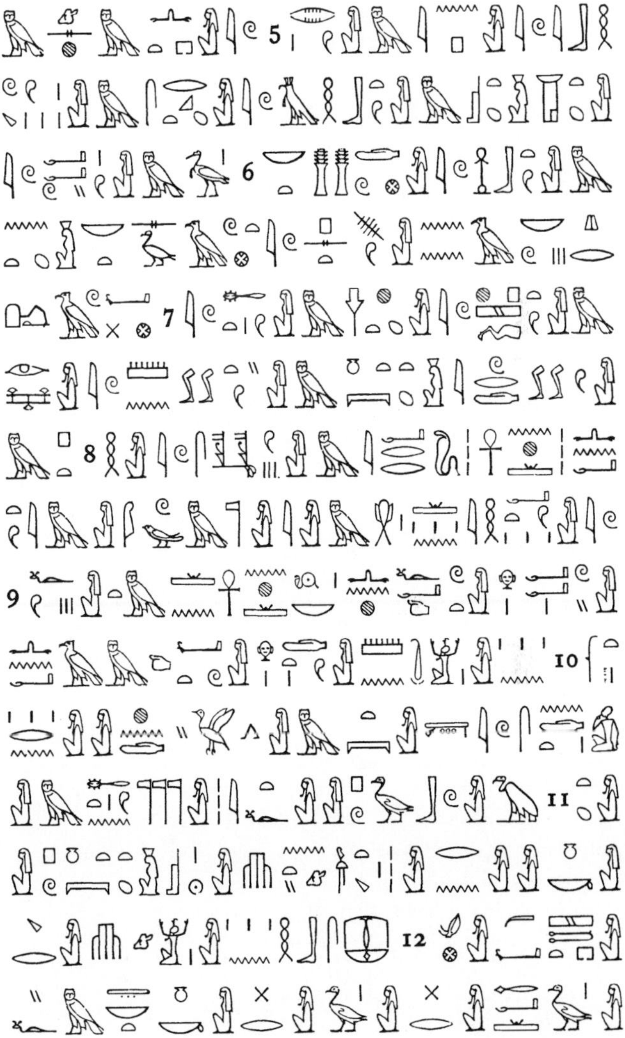

The Book of traversing Eternity.

[Bergmann, *Das Buch vom Durchwandeln der Ewigkeit* (Sitzungsberichte der Kaiserlichen Akad. der Wissensch., Bd. LXXXVI, Jahrg. 1877, Wien, 1877).]

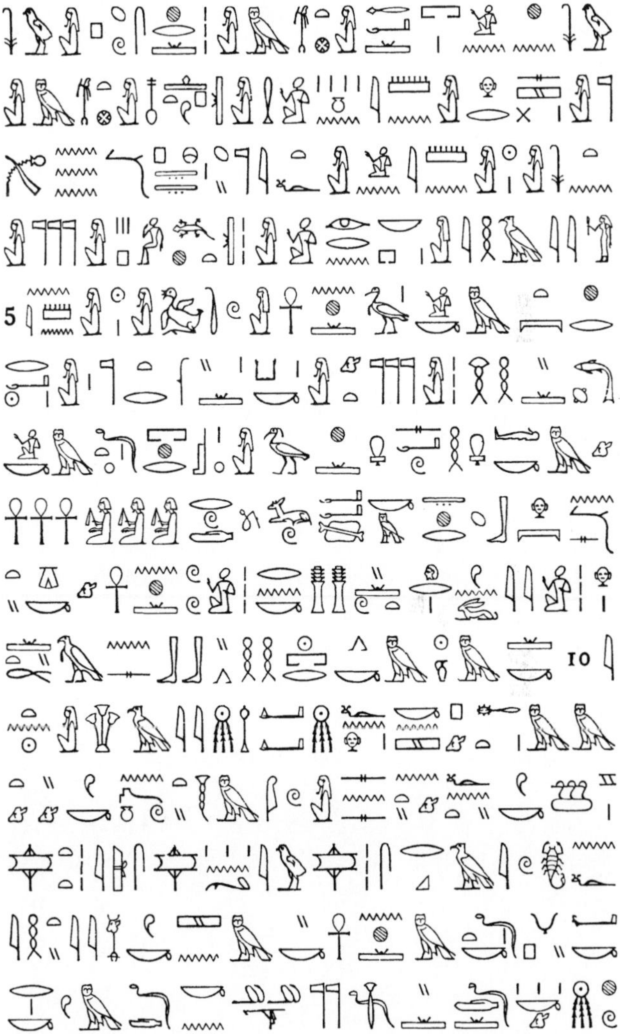

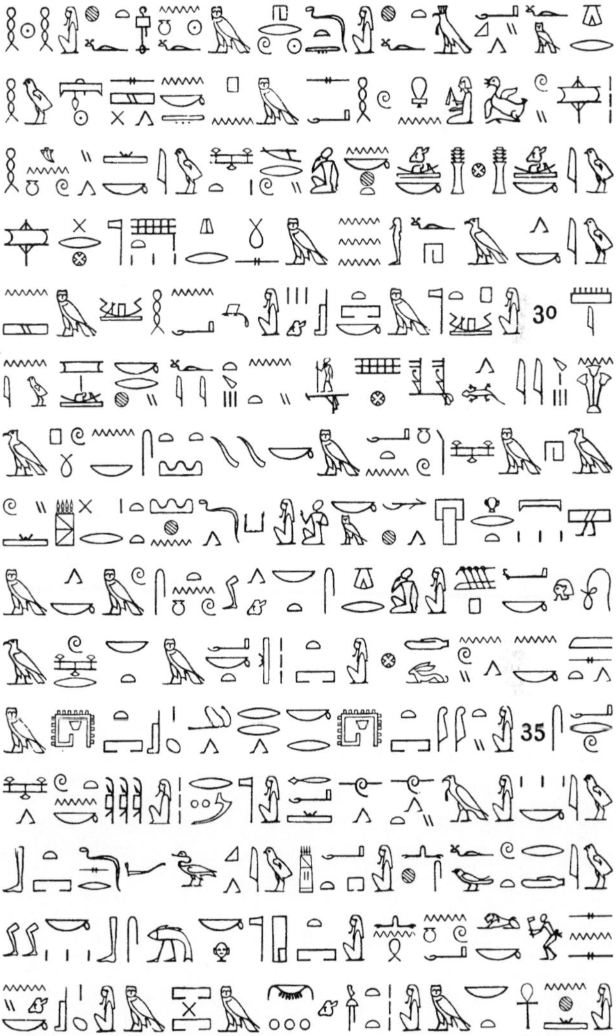

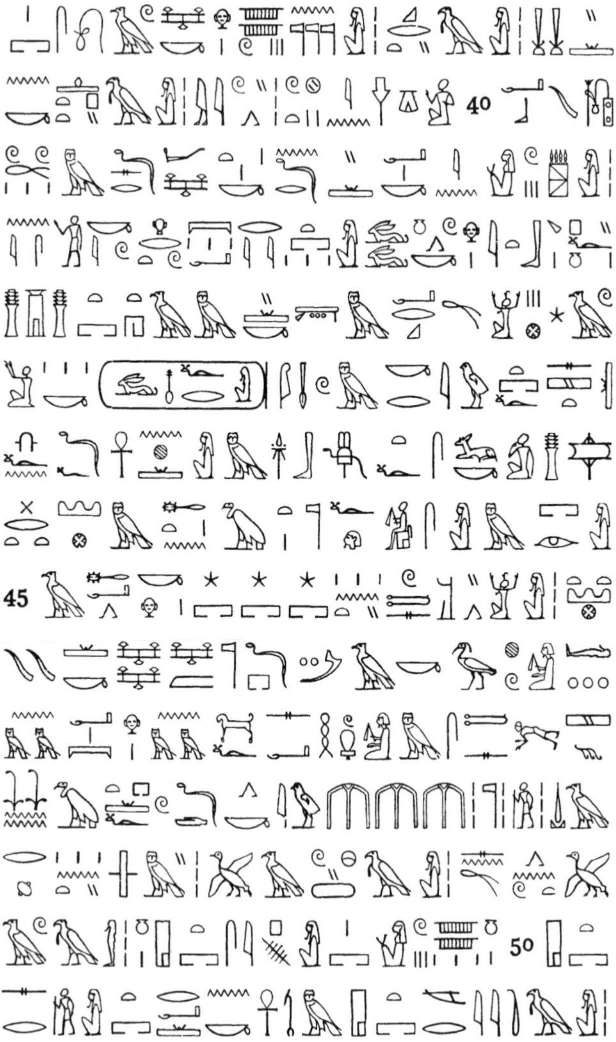

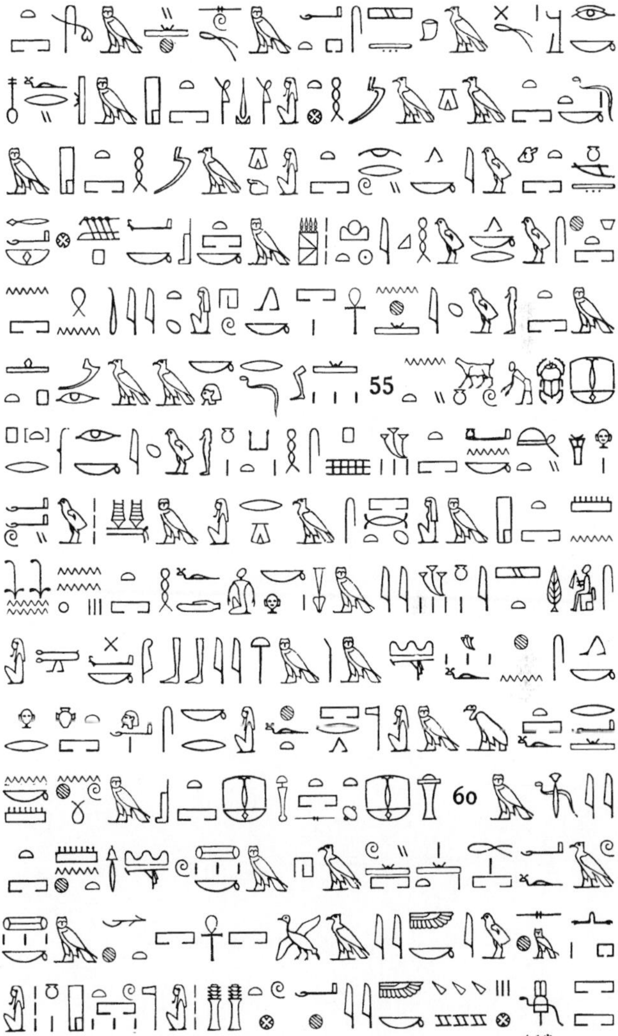
55
60

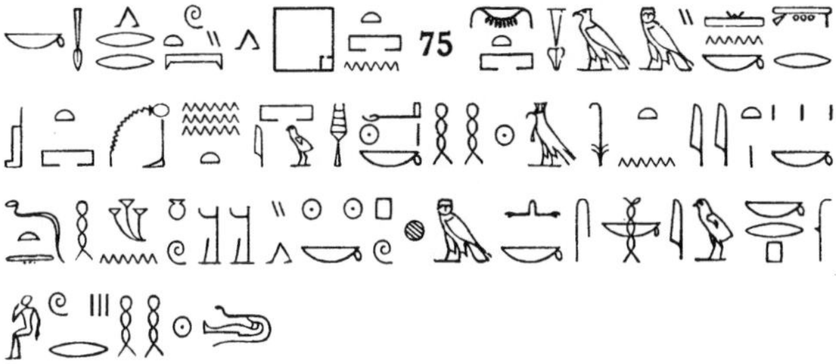

A Shorter Version.

[From a Stele in the Vatican (No. 128 *a* of Marucchi's *Catalogo*); see also Wreszinski, *Aeg. Zeitschr.*, 1909, p. 111 ff.]

1. Nut Åqertet.

11
12
13
14
15
16
(sic)
17

Address to Takherṭ p-seru àbṭiu.

[From British Museum Papyrus, No. 10,112, and see Lieblein, *Que mon nom*, p. 1.]

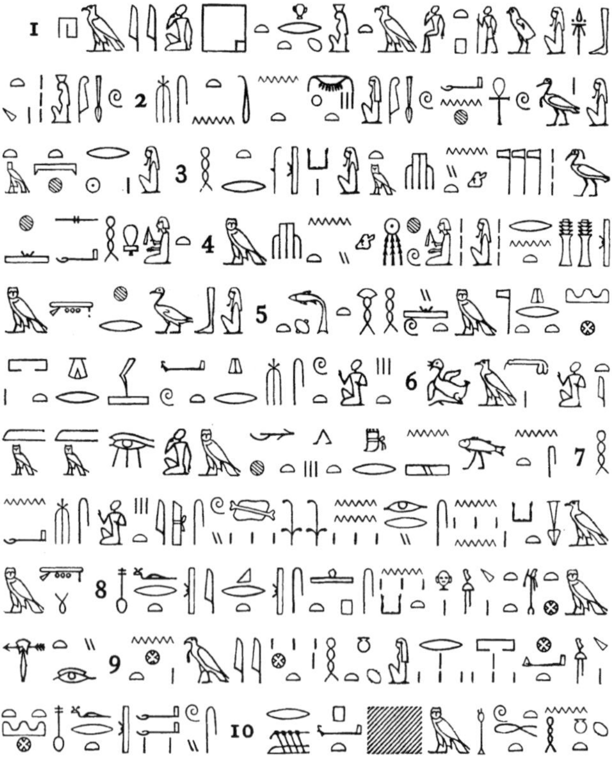

11
12
13
14
15
16
17
18
19
20
21
22

23 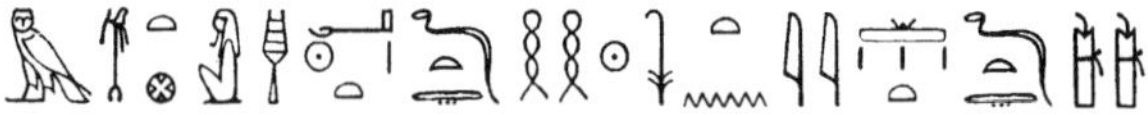

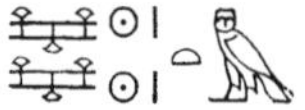 24 . On the back of the papyrus is written : 

A Prayer for the Preservation of the Name.

[From the Pyramid of Pepi II (ed. Maspero, p. 382).]

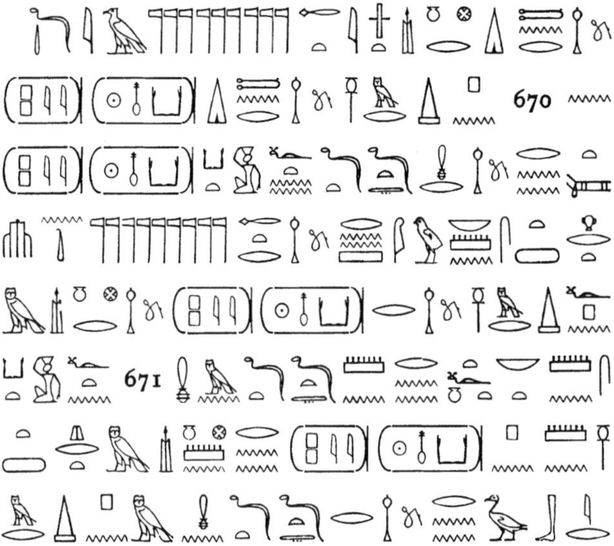

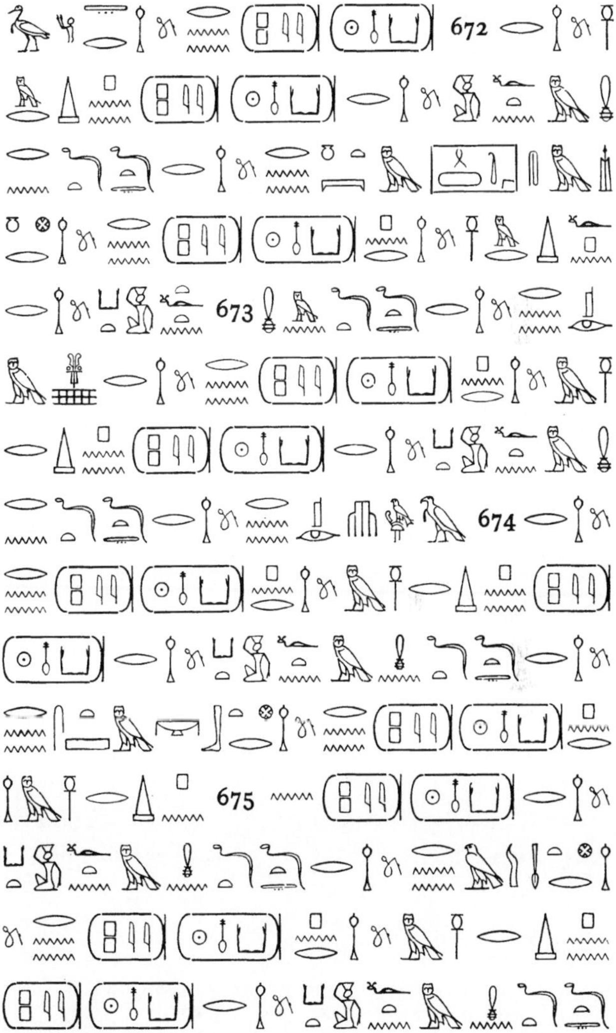
672
673
674
675

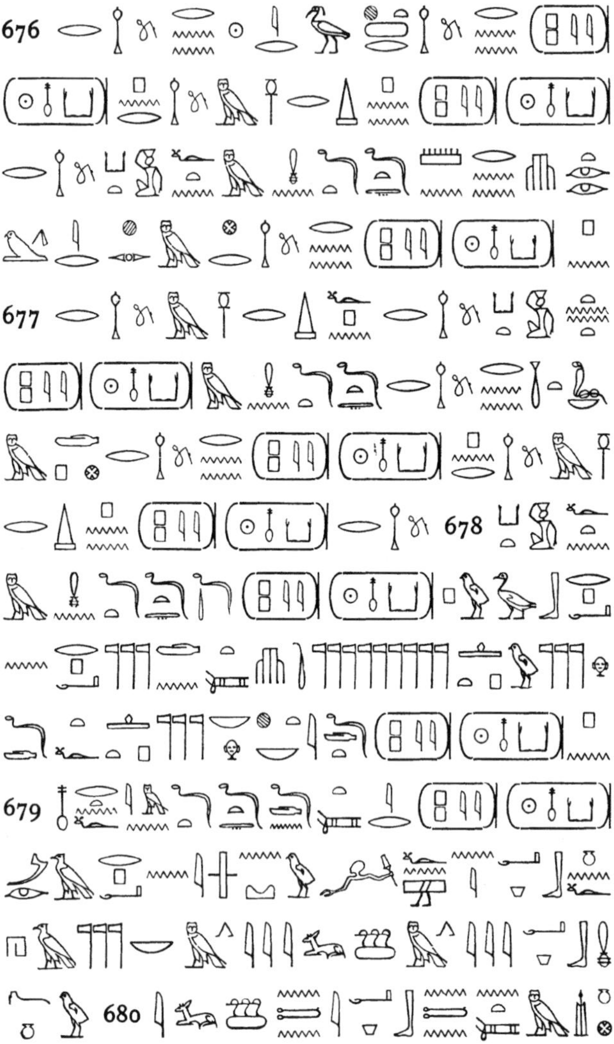
676
677
678
679
680

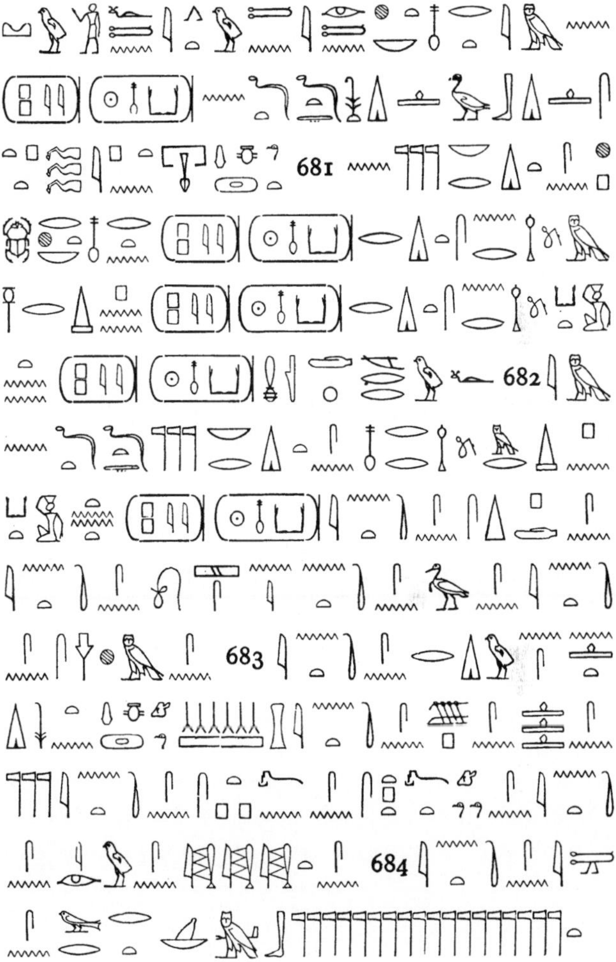
681
682
683
684

Funeral text of Hertu.

[For the hieratic text see Lepsius, *Denkmäler*, VI, 122; and see Lieblein, *Que mon nom*, No. 18).]

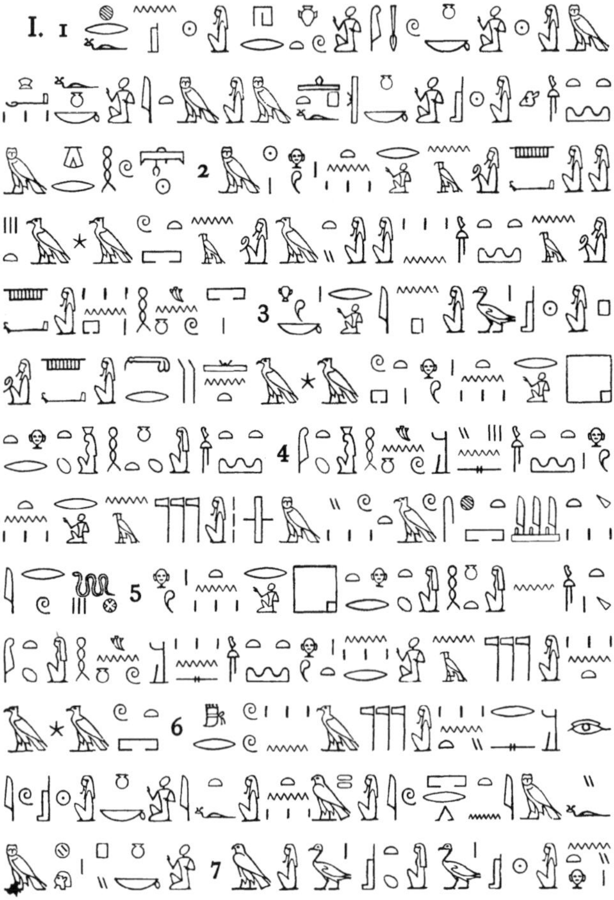

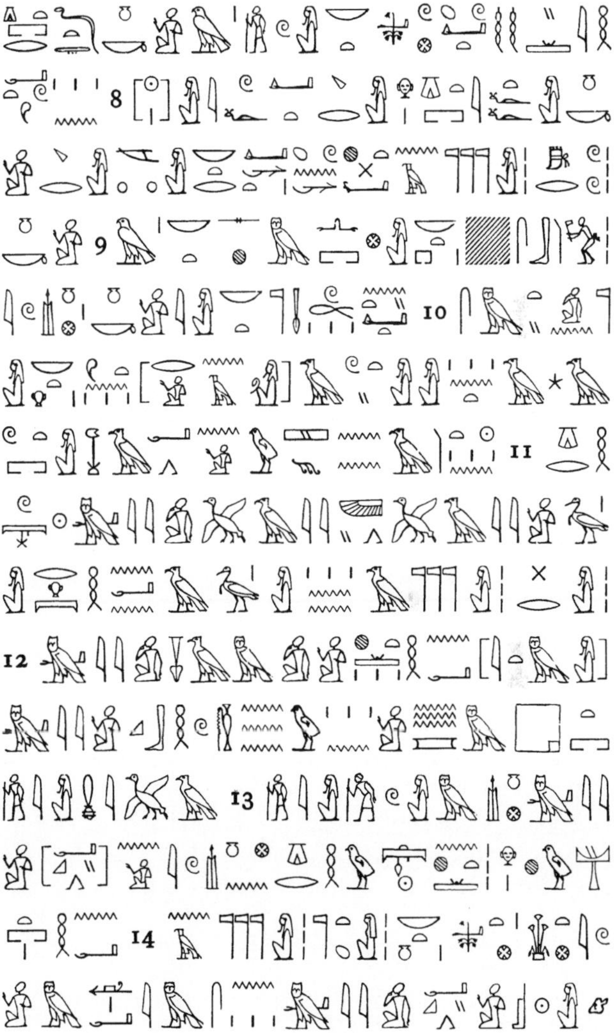

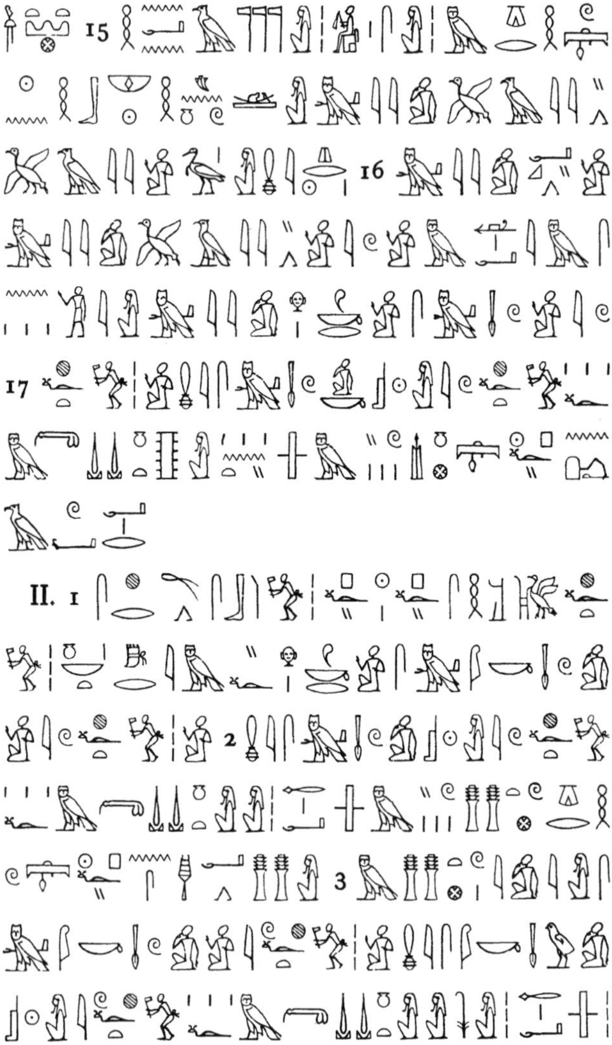
15
16
17
II. 1
2
3

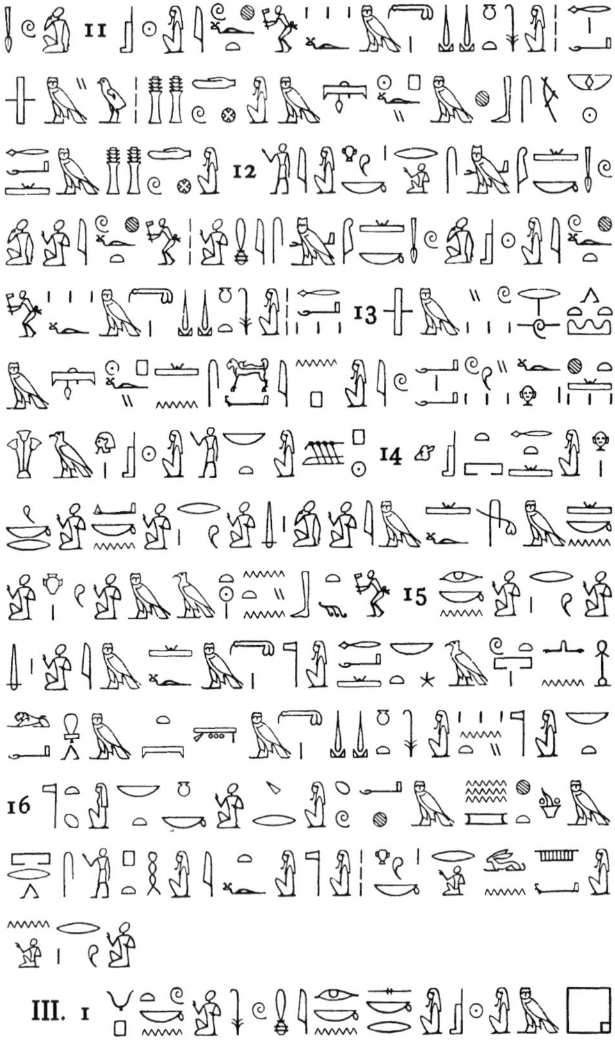

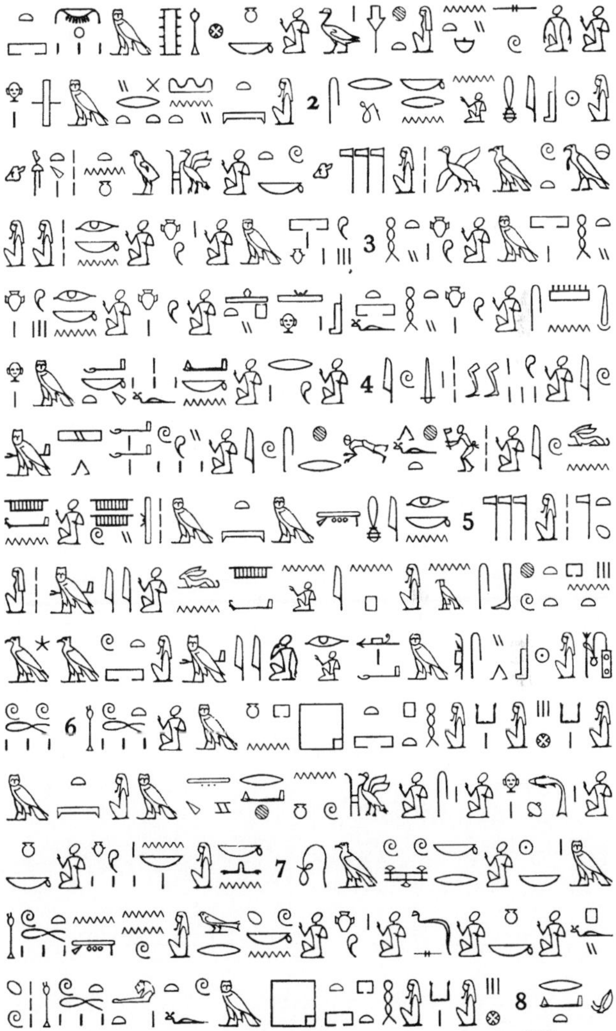

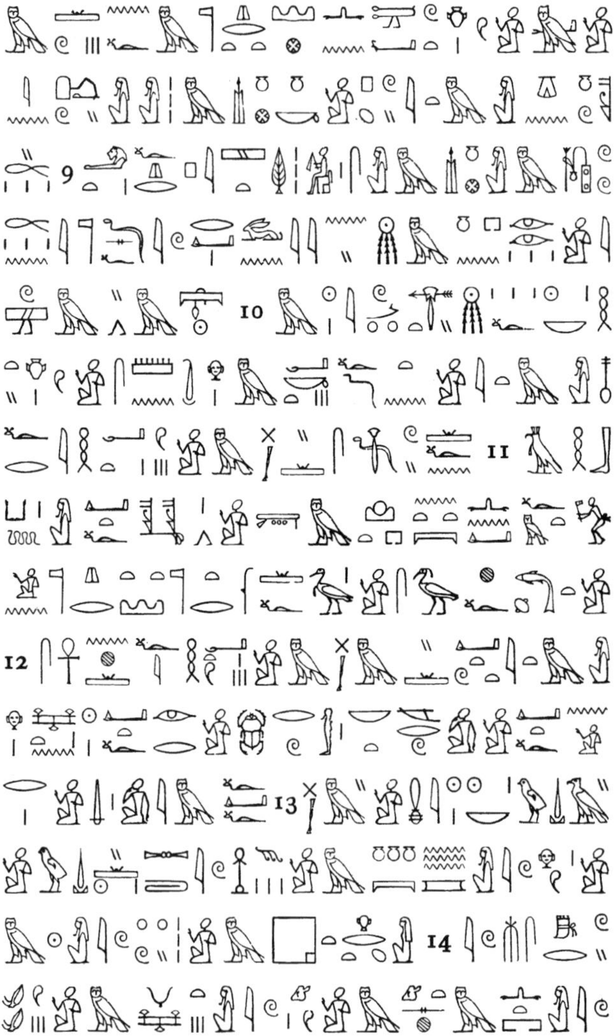
9
10
11
12
13
14

[hieroglyphic text - line 1]

[hieroglyphic text - line 2] 6

[hieroglyphic text - line 3]

[hieroglyphic text - line 4]

7 [hieroglyphic text - line 5]

[hieroglyphic text - line 6]

8 [hieroglyphic text - line 7]

[hieroglyphic text - line 8]

9 [hieroglyphic text - line 9]

[hieroglyphic text - line 10]

10 [hieroglyphic text - line 11]

[hieroglyphic text - line 12]

11 [hieroglyphic text - line 13]

[hieroglyphic text - line 14] 12

[hieroglyphic text - line 15]

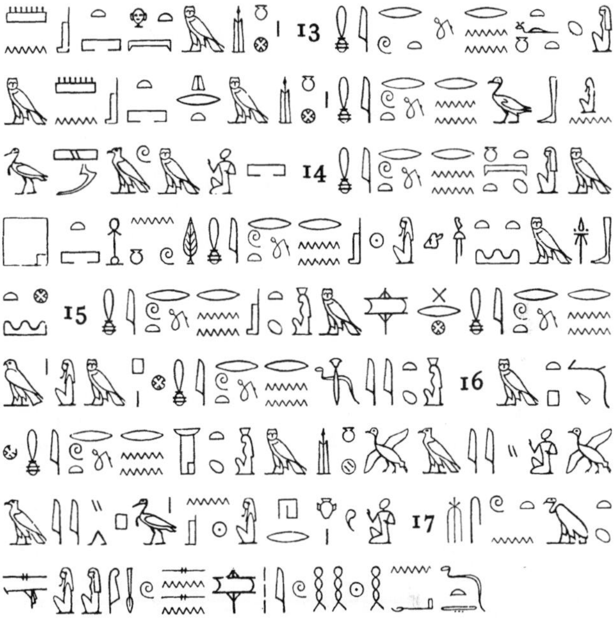

The Funeral Text of Ānkh-f-en-ḥetemti, an Utcheb Priest.

[From a Papyrus in the Egyptian Museum, Cairo (Lieblein, *Que mon nom*, plate XVII ff).]

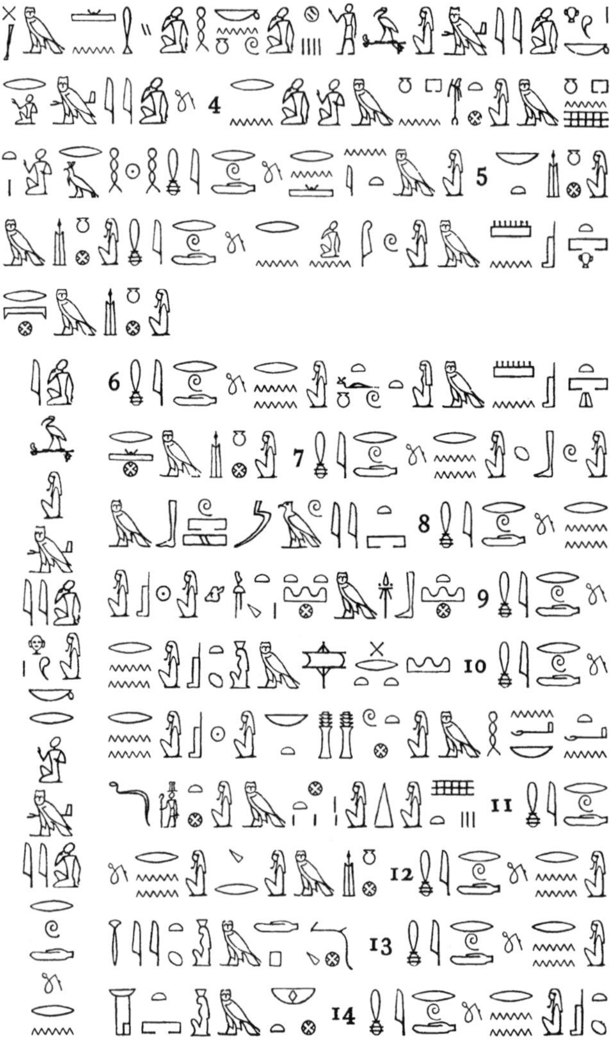

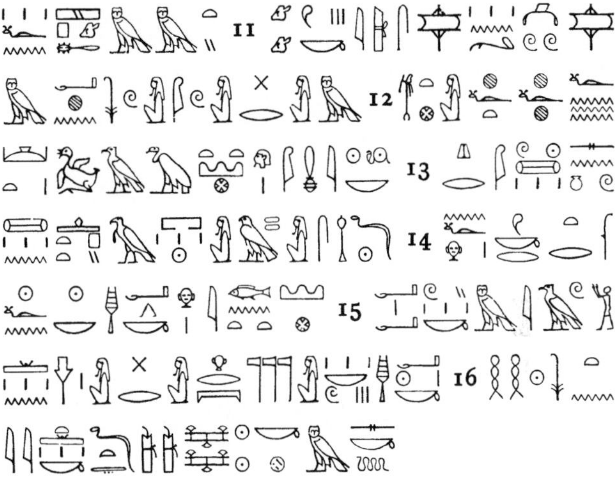

Specimen Chapters of the Book of the Dead from Recensions of Various Periods.

A. I. Version of the Chapter XLII. VIth dynasty.

II. Versions of Chapters XVII, XXIV, XXIX, XXXIX, XLIII, LII, LIV, LXII, and miscellaneous Chapters. XIth and XIIth dynasties.

III. Versions of Chapters XXVI, XXX B and LXIV, from an electrotype in the British Museum (No. 29,553). XXVIth dynasty.

IV. Versions of Chapters I, II, IX, X, XXIII, XXIV, XXVI, XXVIII, XXX B, XXXI, XLIV, XLVII, LVI, LIX, LXIII A, LXVIII, LXXI, LXXXIX, XCI, CV, CLIV, from the coffin of Basa-en-Mut in the British Museum (No. 22,940). XXVIth dynasty, or later.

B. I. Funerary text from the Sarcophagus of Queen Ānkhnes-neferȧb-Rā in the British Museum (No. 811). XXVIth dynasty.

II. Version of a text of the VIth dynasty found in the Tomb of Peṭā-Ȧmen-ȧp. XXVIth dynasty.

A. I.

Chapter XLII.

Version of the Ancient Empire (Pyramid of Pepi I, line 565 ff).

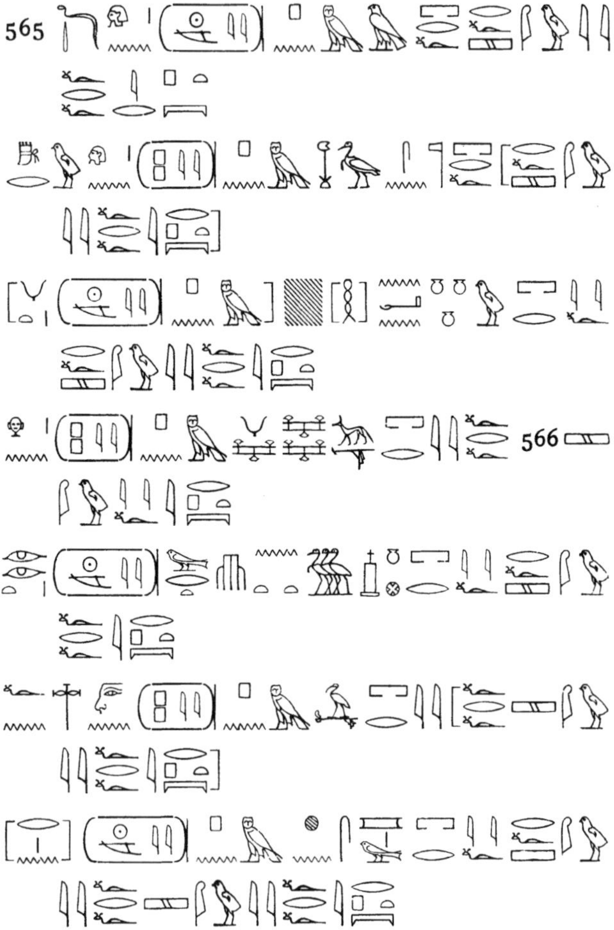

567
568
569

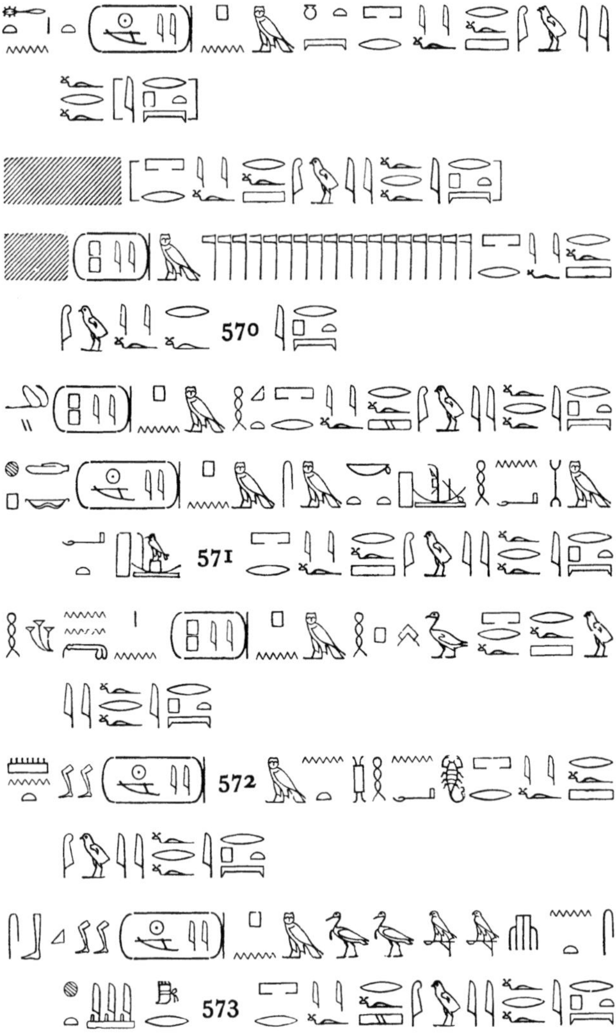
570
571
572
573

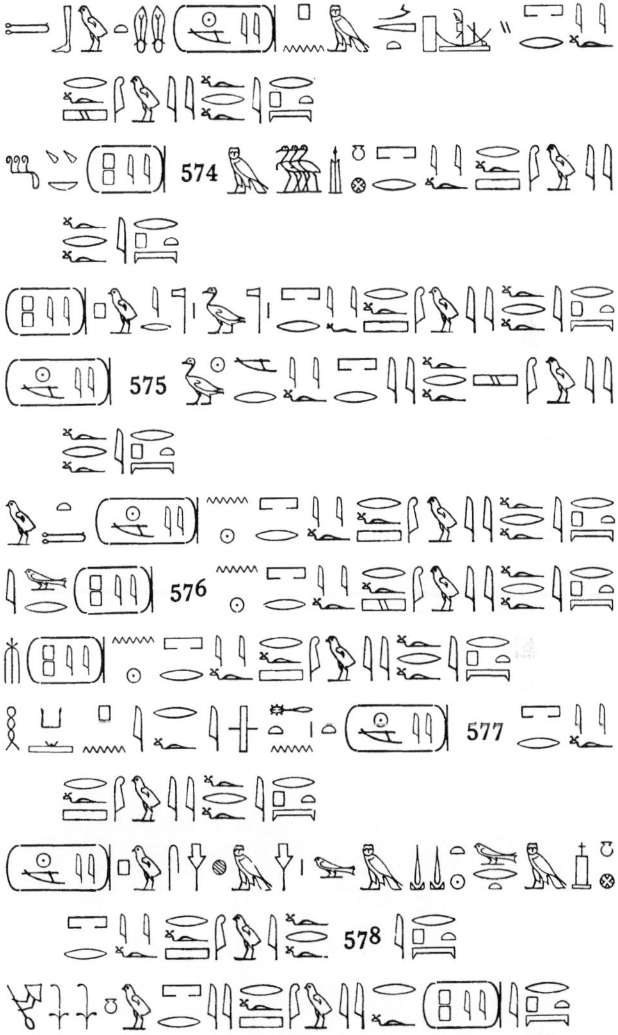
574
575
576
577
578

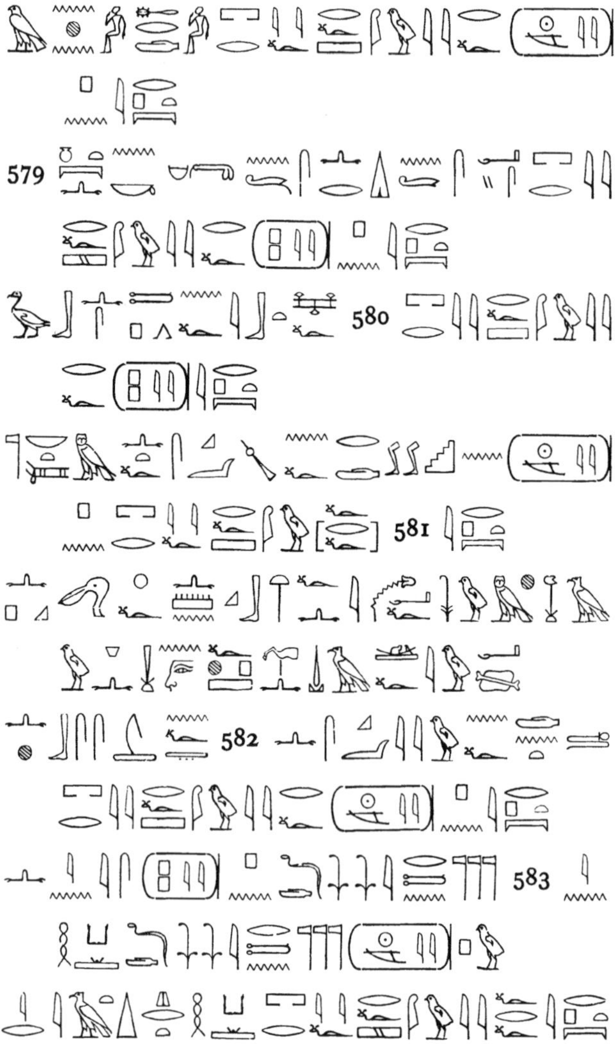
579
580
581
582
583

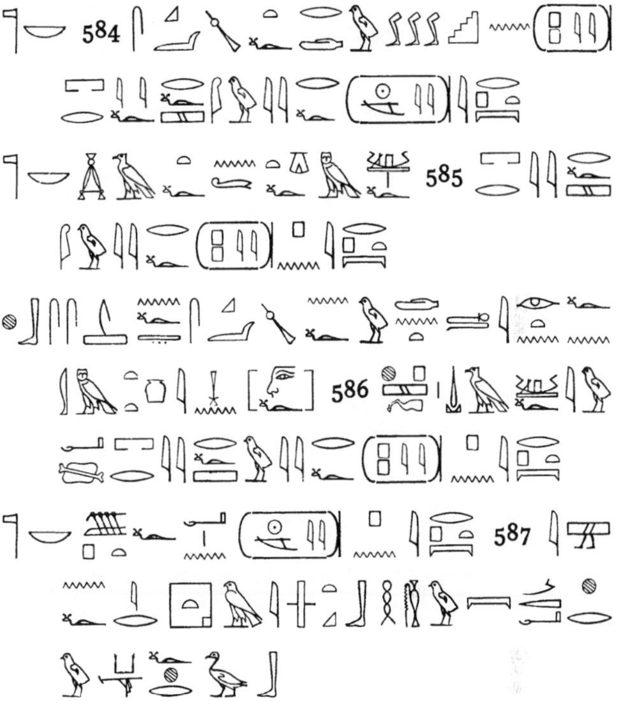

A. II.

Chapter XVII.

1. [From the tomb of Ḥer (Maspero, *Mémoires*, tome I, p. 142).]

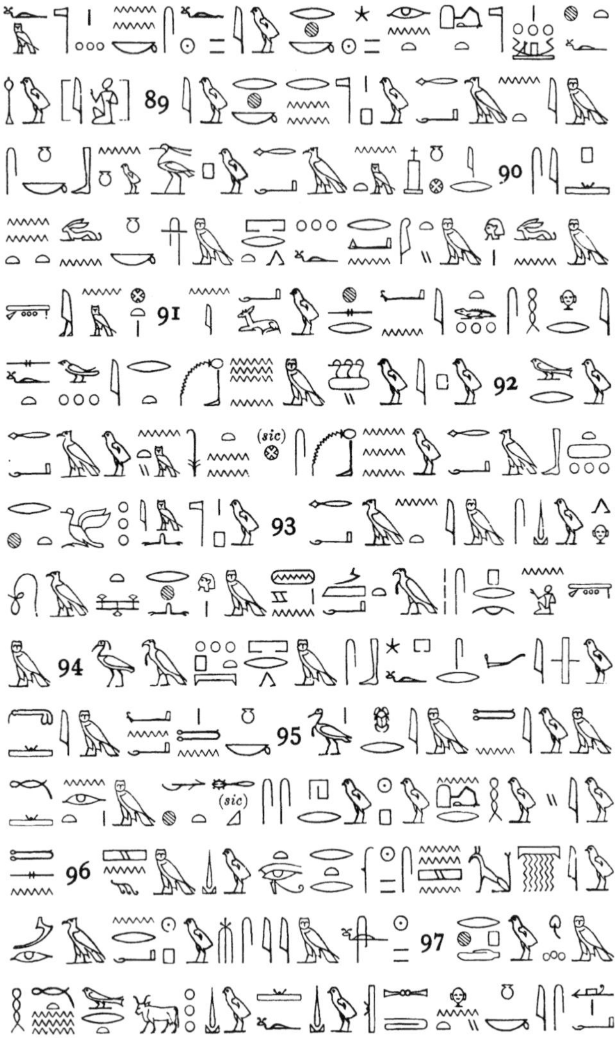
89
90
91
92
(sic)
93
94
95
(sic)
96
97

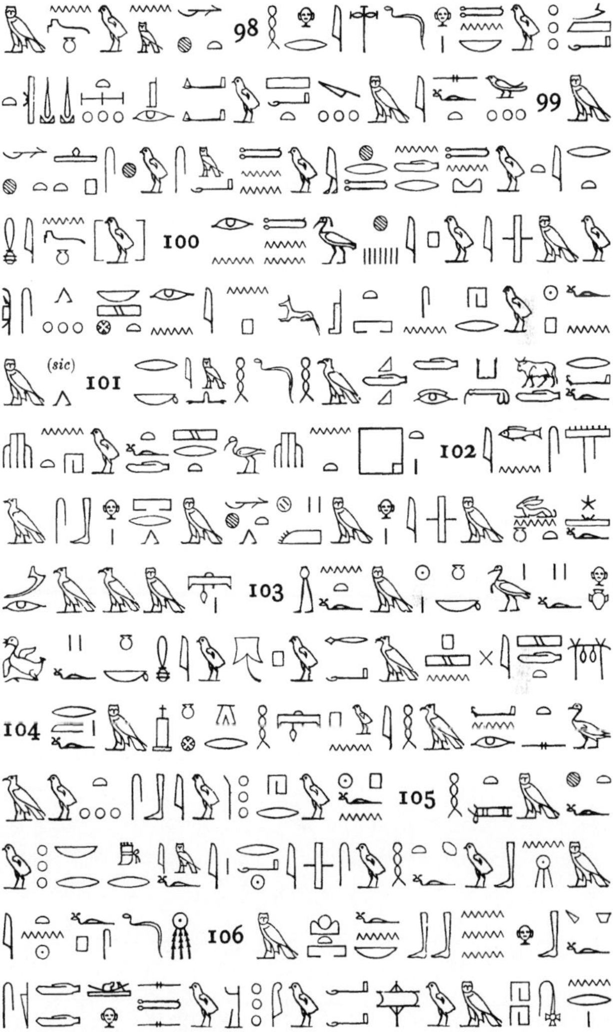
98
99
100
(sic)
101
102
103
104
105
106

107 

2. [From the sarcophagus of Ḥer (Maspero, *Mémoires*, tome I, p. 167).]

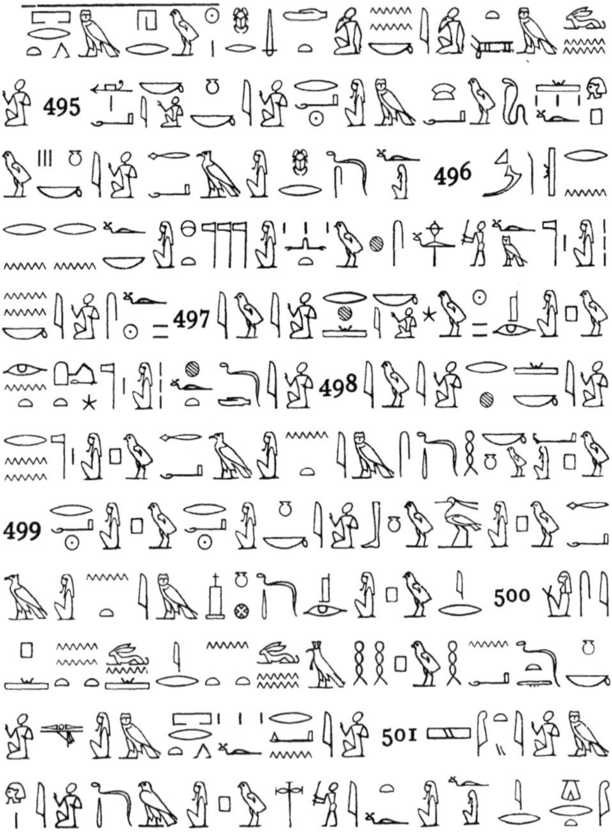

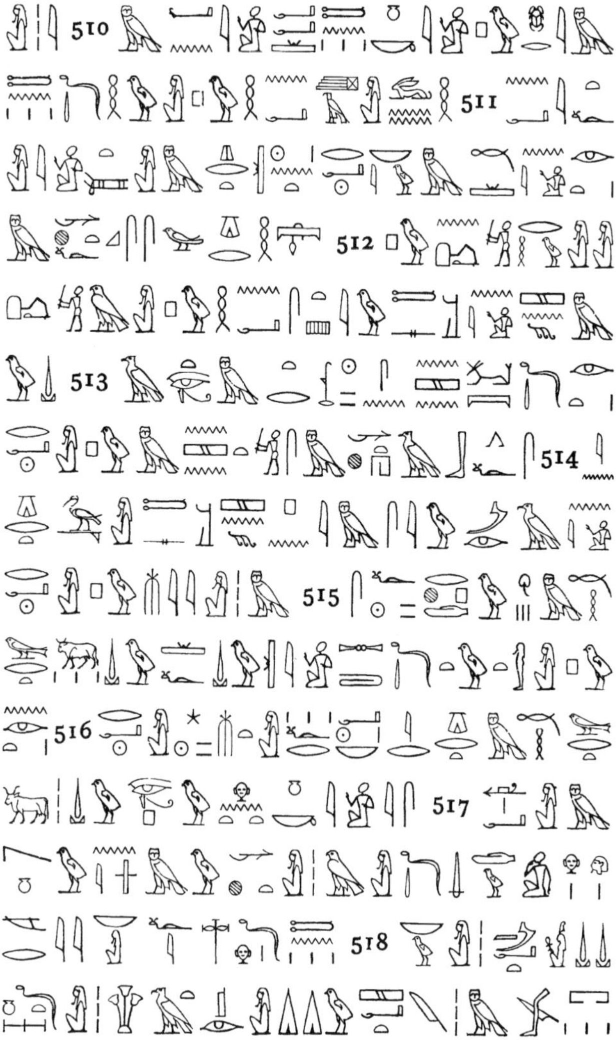
510
511
512
513
514
515
516
517
518

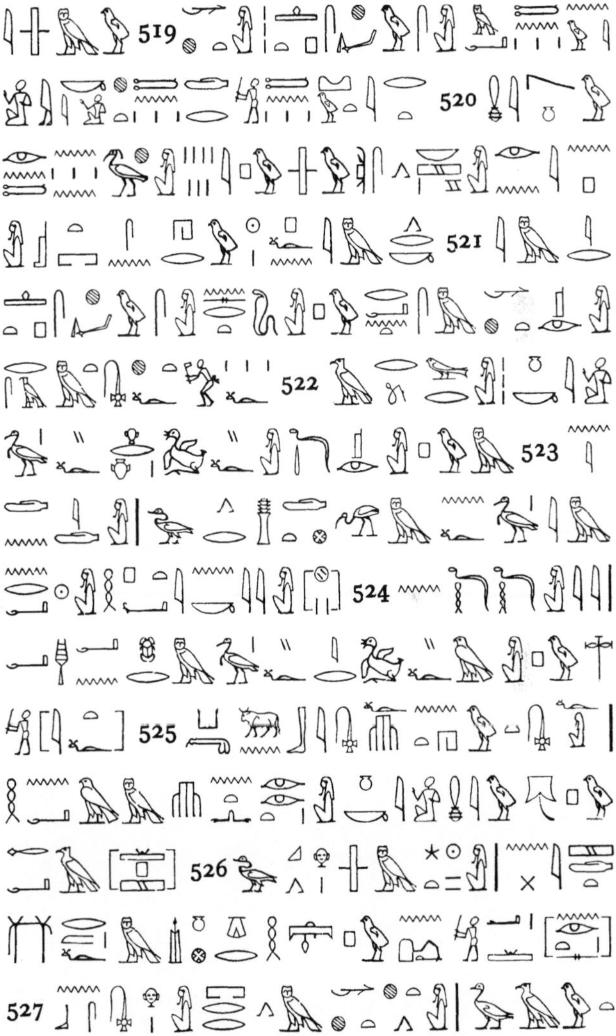
519
520
521
522
523
524
525
526
527

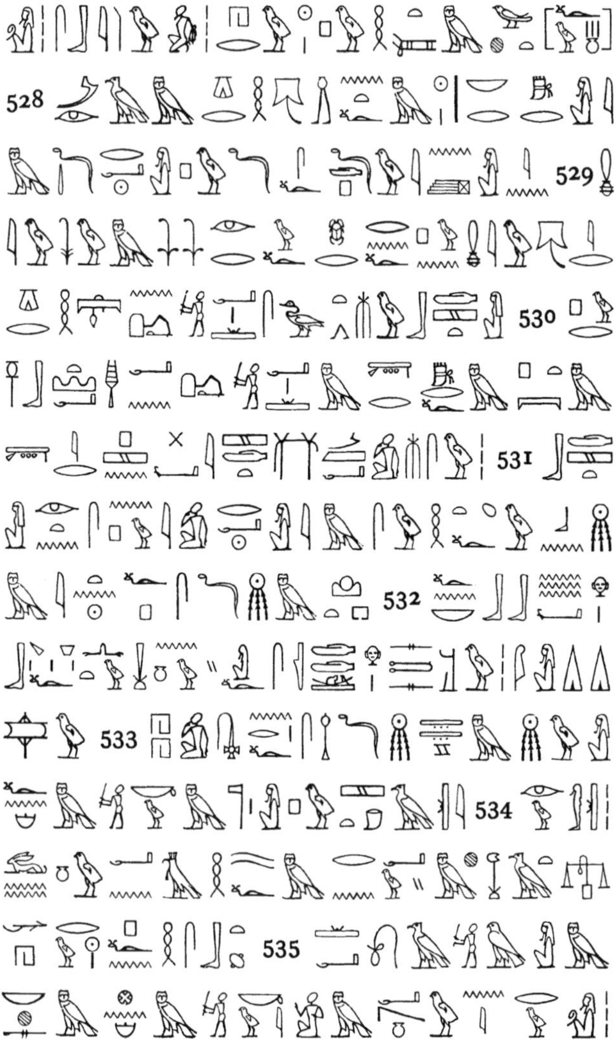
528
529
530
531
532
533
534
535

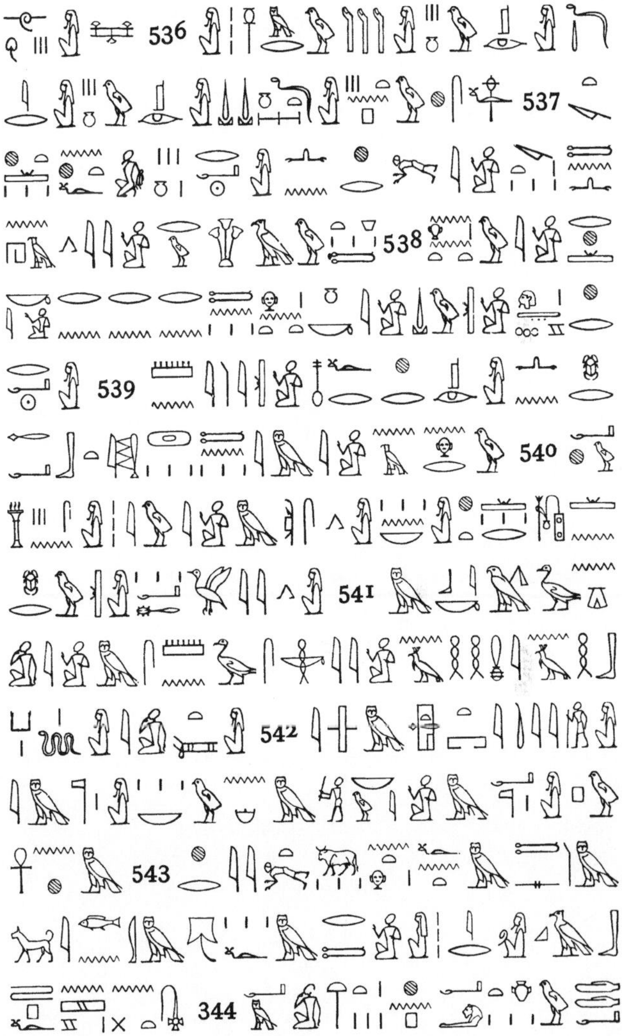
536
537
538
539
540
541
542
543
344

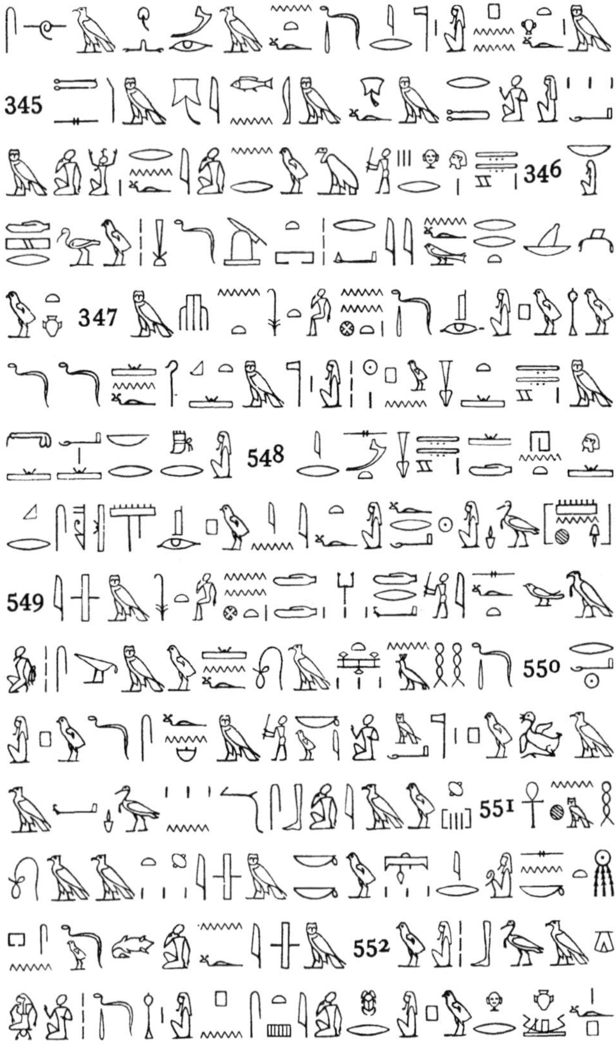

345
346
347
548
549
550
551
552

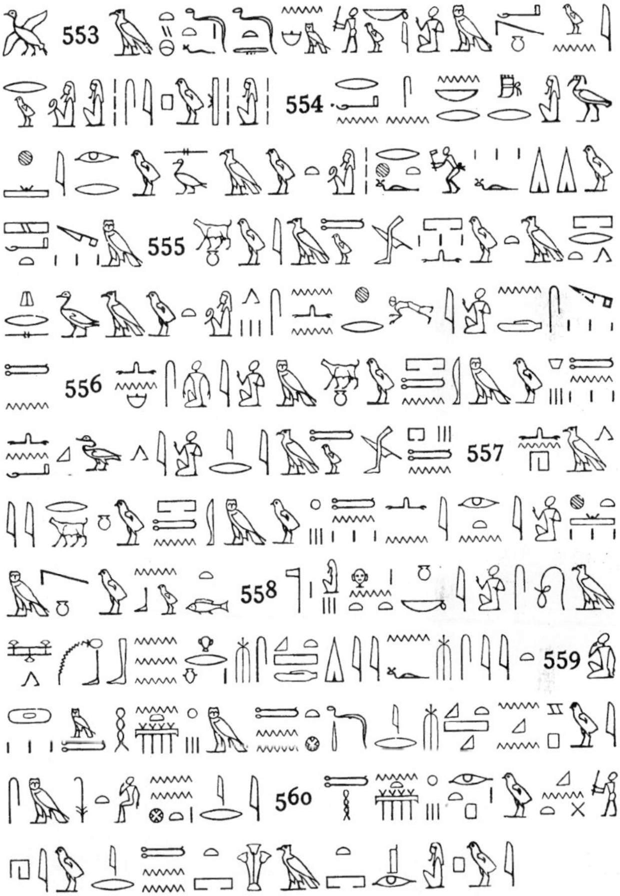
553
554
555
556
557
558
559
560

3. [From the coffin of Ḥer  (Maspero, *Mémoires*, tome I, p. 210).]

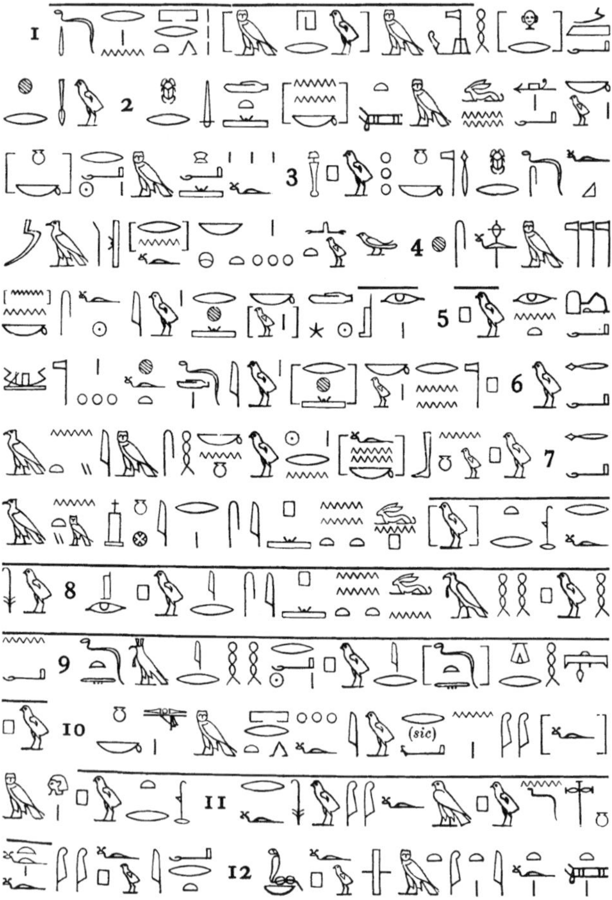

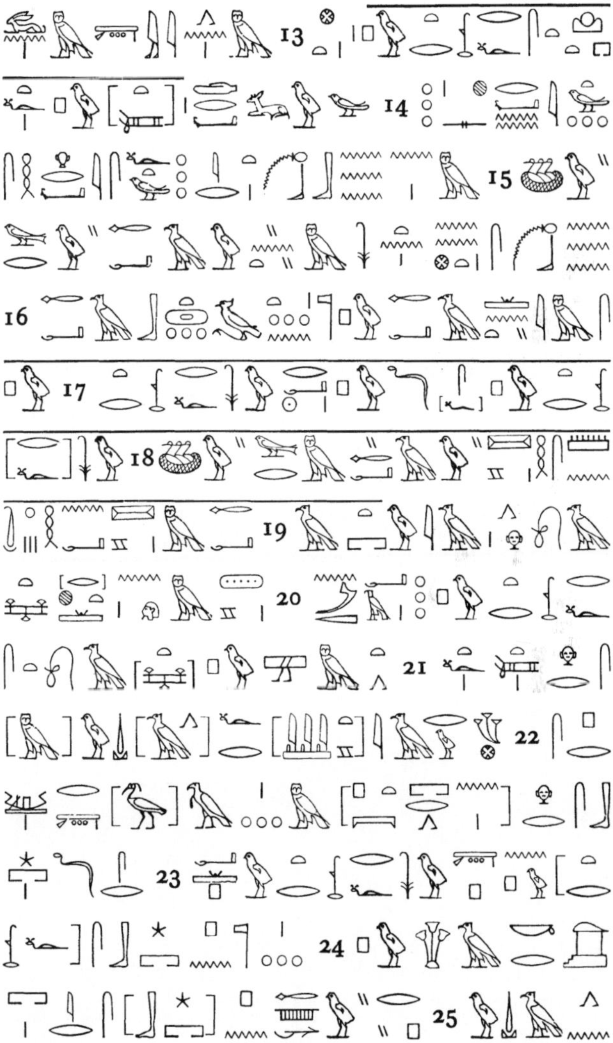

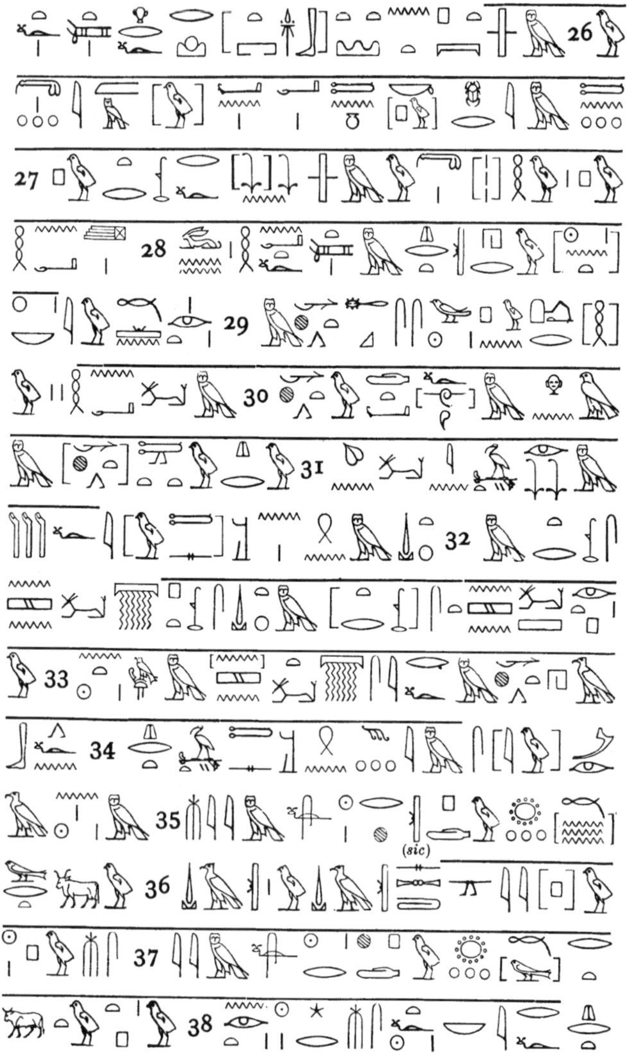
26
27
28
29
30
31
32
33
34
35
(sic)
36
37
38

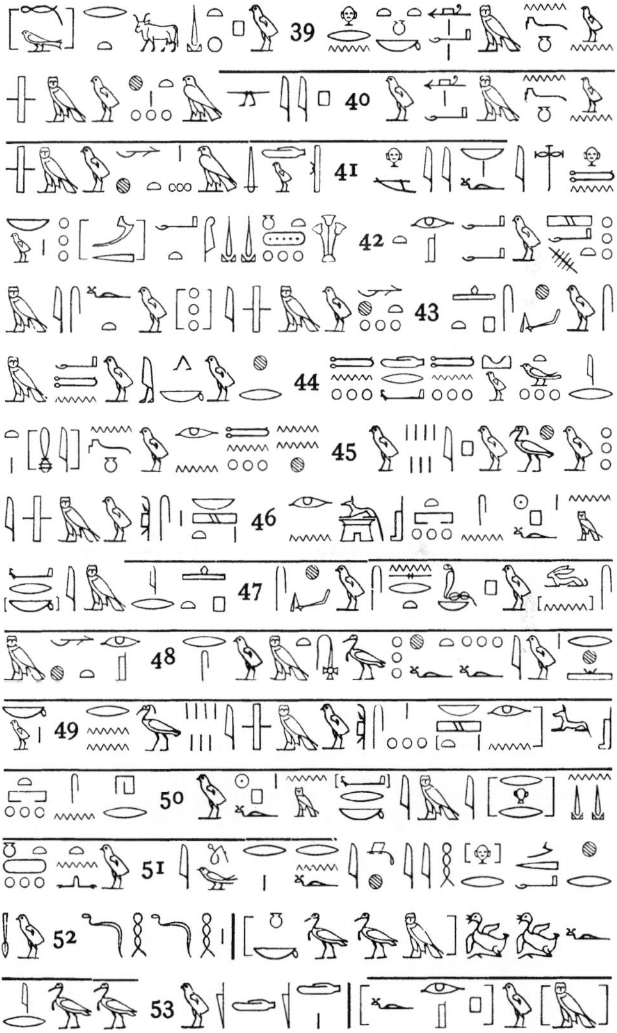
39
40
41
42
43
44
45
46
47
48
49
50
51
52
53

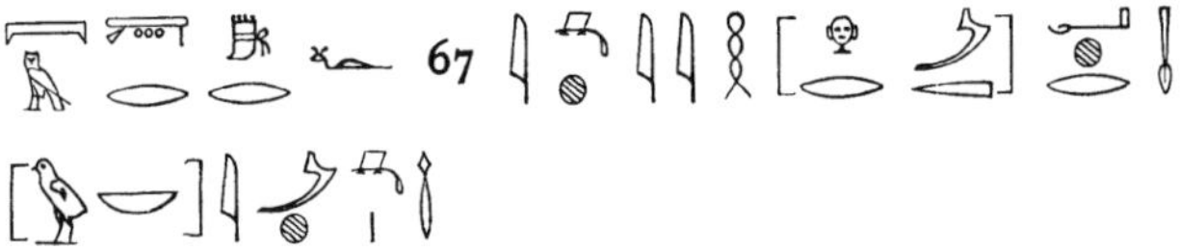

4. [From the coffin of Sat-Bast (Maspero, *Mémoires*, I, p. 218).]

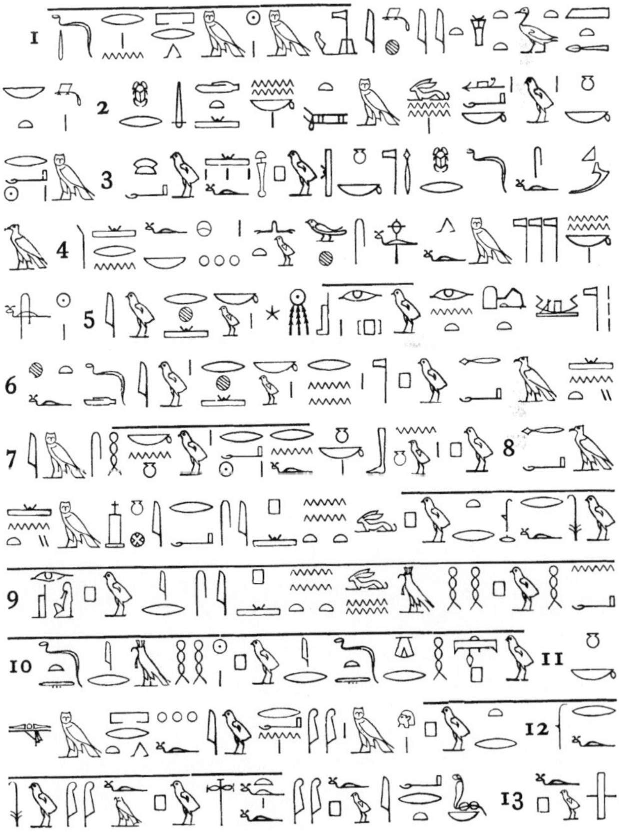

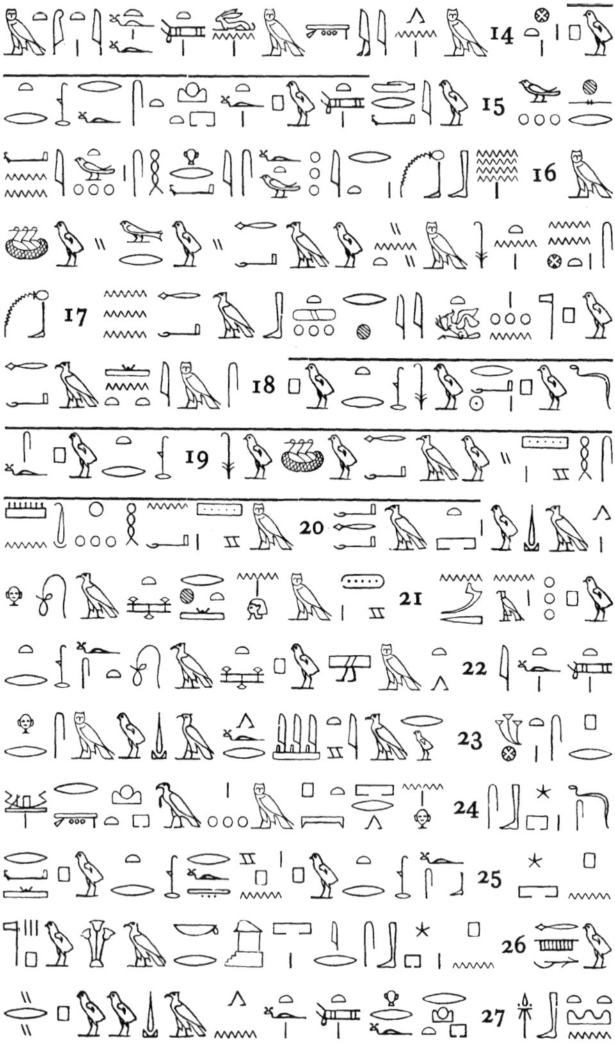
14
15
16
17
18
19
20
21
22
23
24
25
26
27

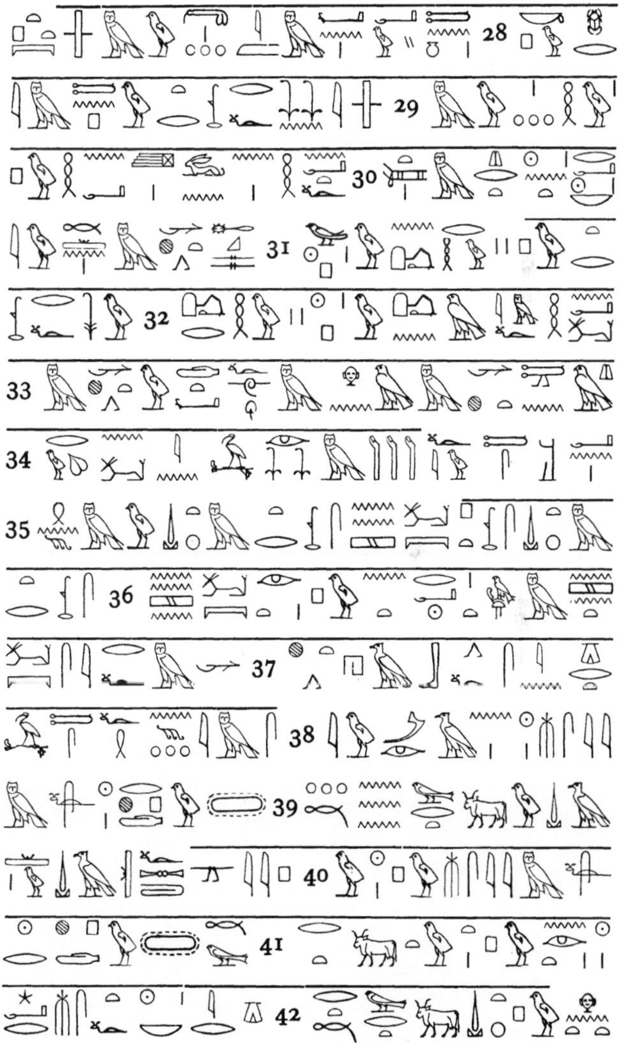
28
29
30
31
32
33
34
35
36
37
38
39
40
41
42

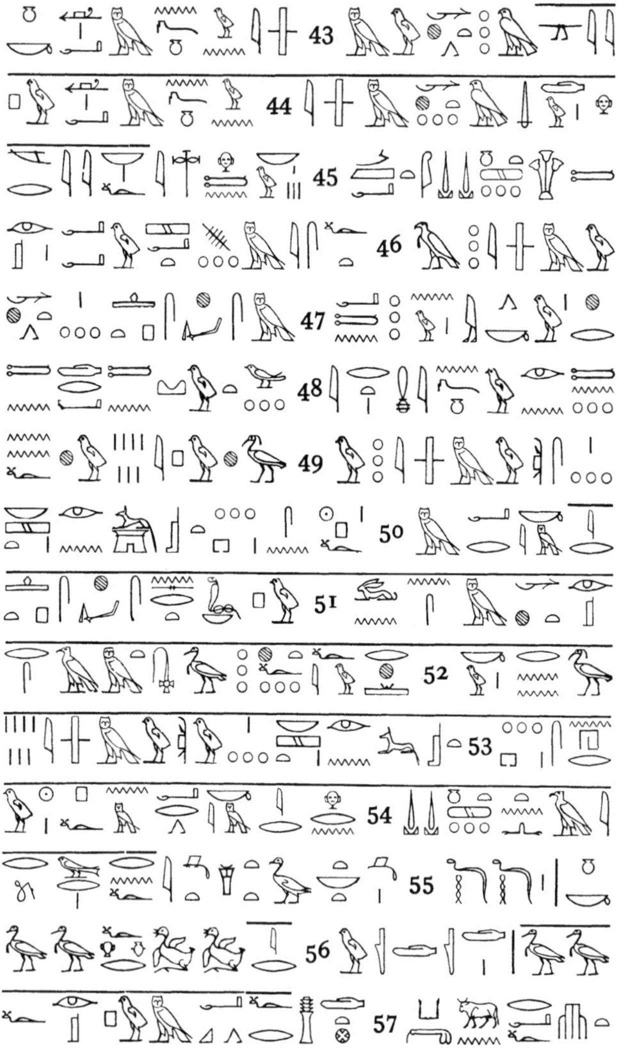

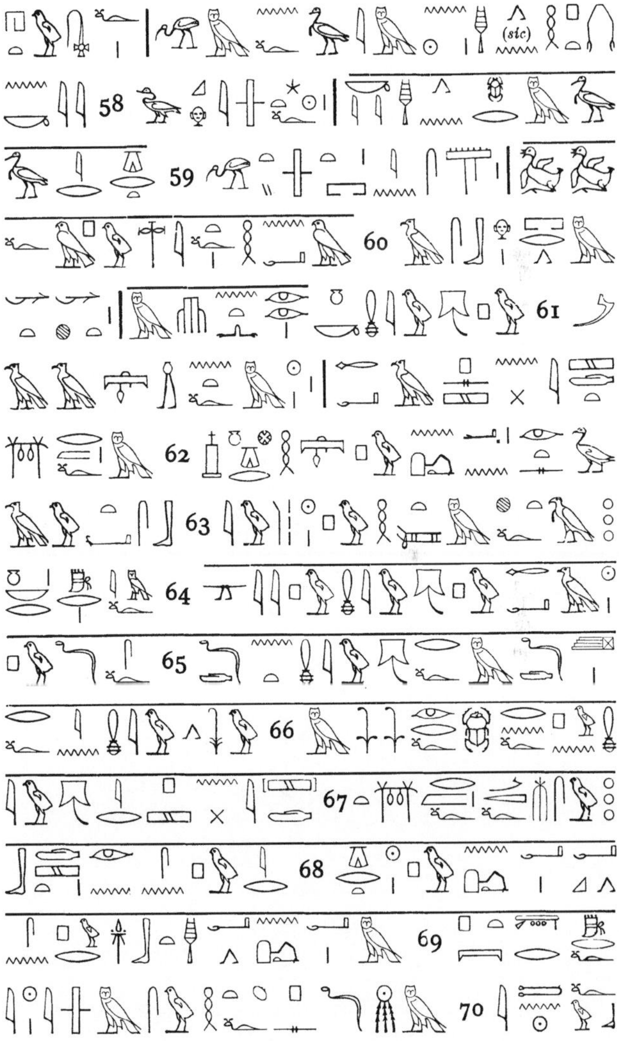
(sic)
58
59
60
61
62
63
64
65
66
67
68
69
70

5. Of bringing spells (Chapter XXIV).

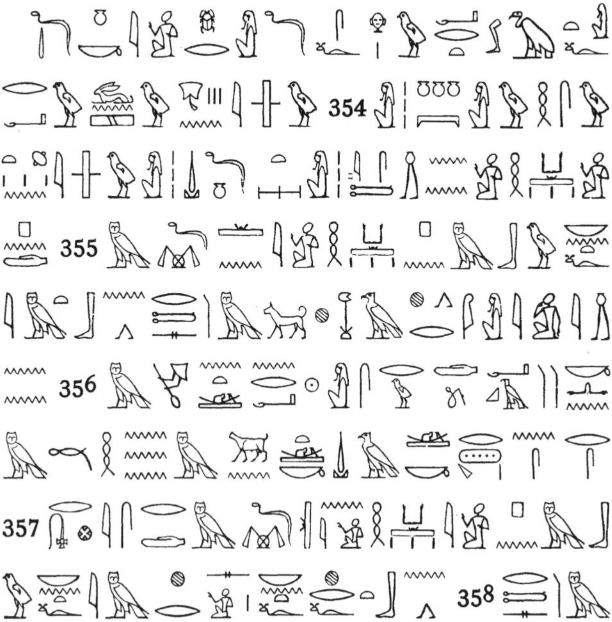

6. Of not letting the heart of a man be carried away (Chapter XXIX).

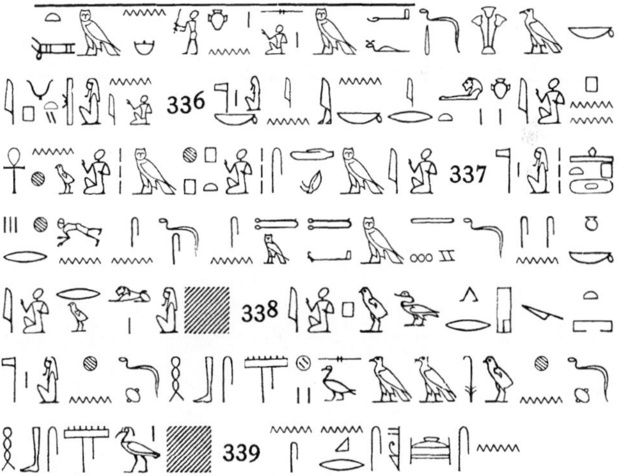

7. Of not letting the heart of a man be taken away (compare Chapter XXIX).

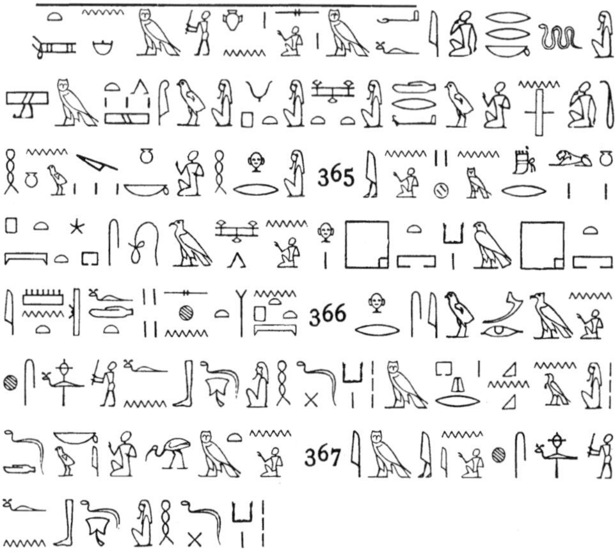

Of not letting the head of a man be cut off (Chapter XLIII).

[hieroglyphic text line with 370]

[hieroglyphic text line]

[hieroglyphic text line with 371]

[hieroglyphic text line]

8. OF NOT EATING FILTH (CHAPTER LII).

[hieroglyphic text line]

[hieroglyphic text line with 395]

[hieroglyphic text line with 396]

[hieroglyphic text line]

[hieroglyphic text line with 397]

[hieroglyphic text line with 398]

[hieroglyphic text line]

[hieroglyphic text line with 399]

[hieroglyphic text line]

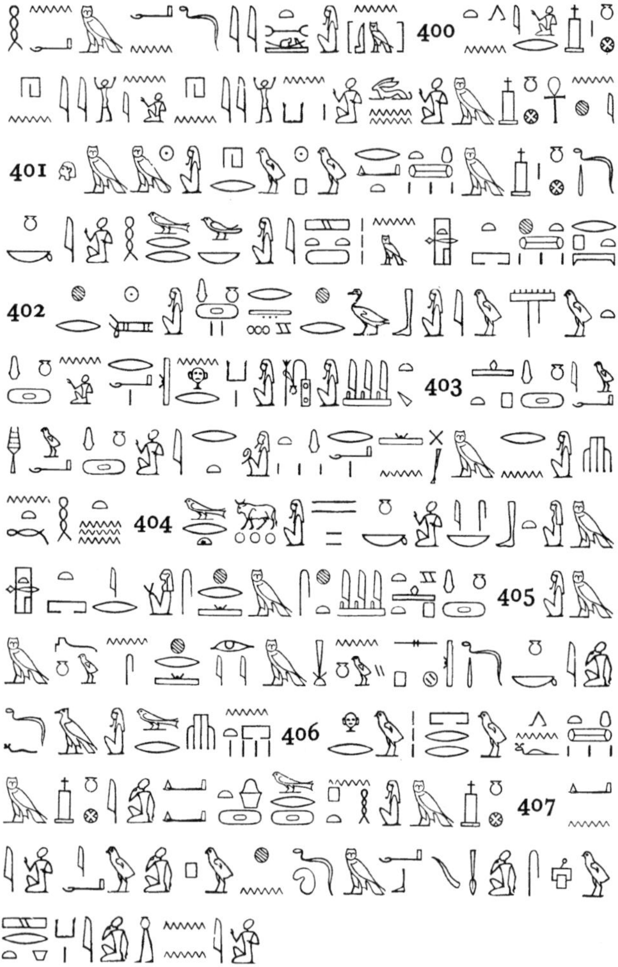

9. Of not eating filth.

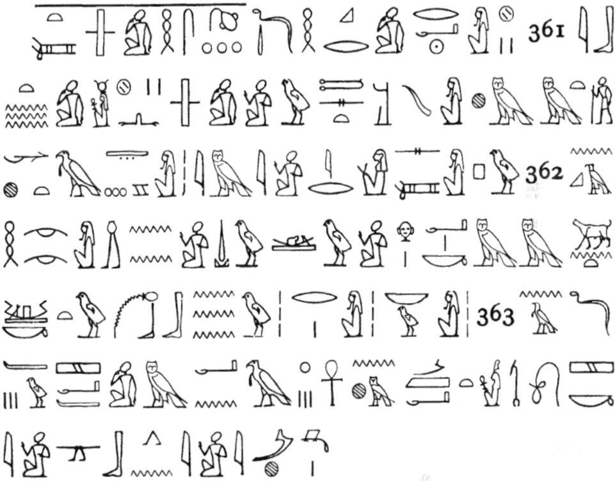

10. Of living in the air, of smelling the air, etc. (Chapter LIV).

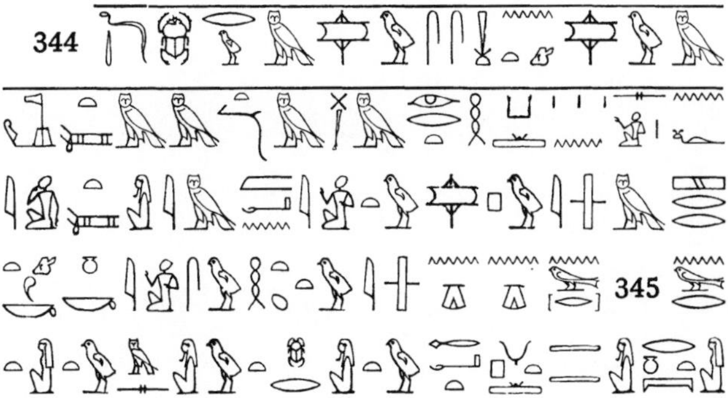

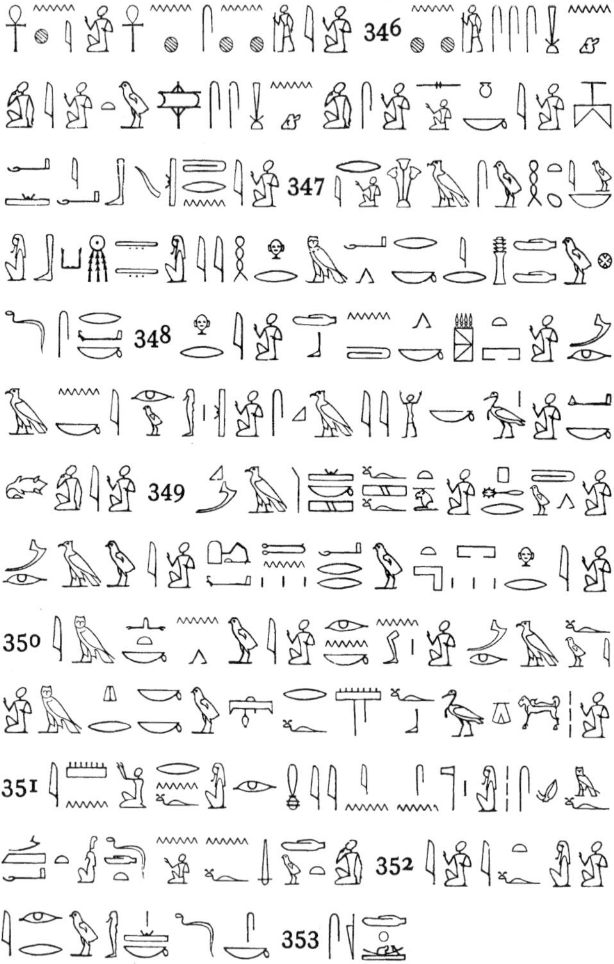
346
347
348
349
350
351
352
353

11. Of having power over water (Chapter LXII).

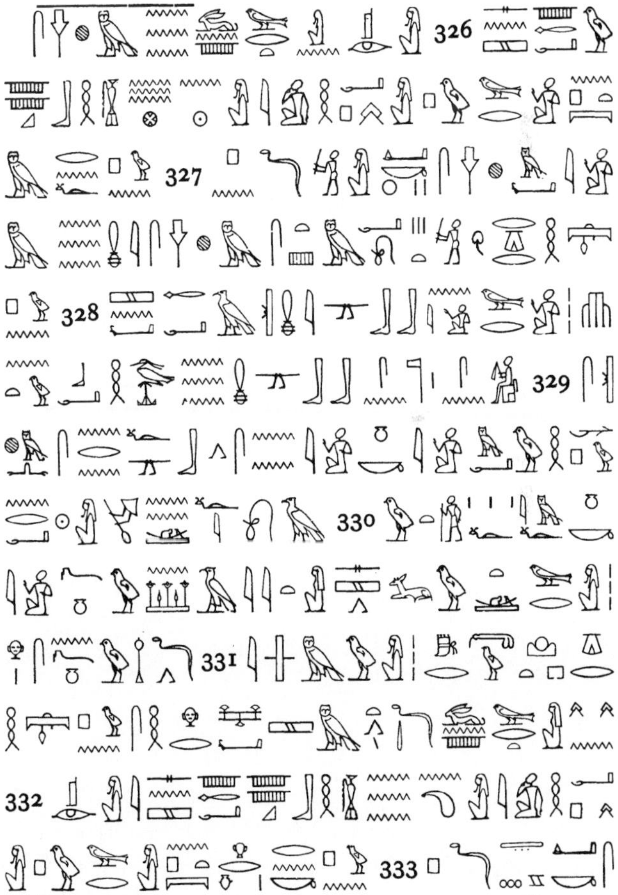

12. Of having power over clean water, etc.

301

302

303

304 305

306

307

308

309

310 311

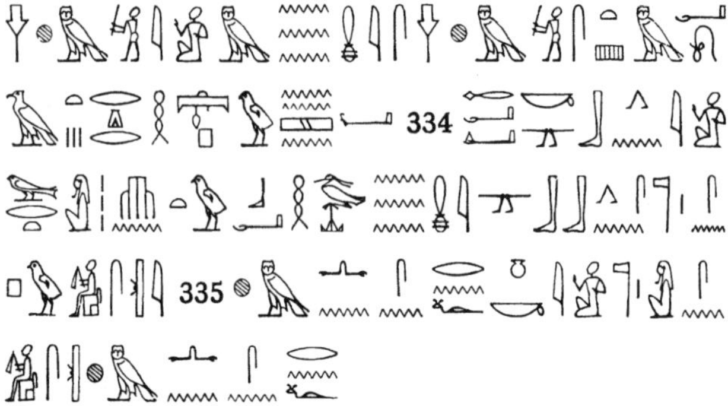

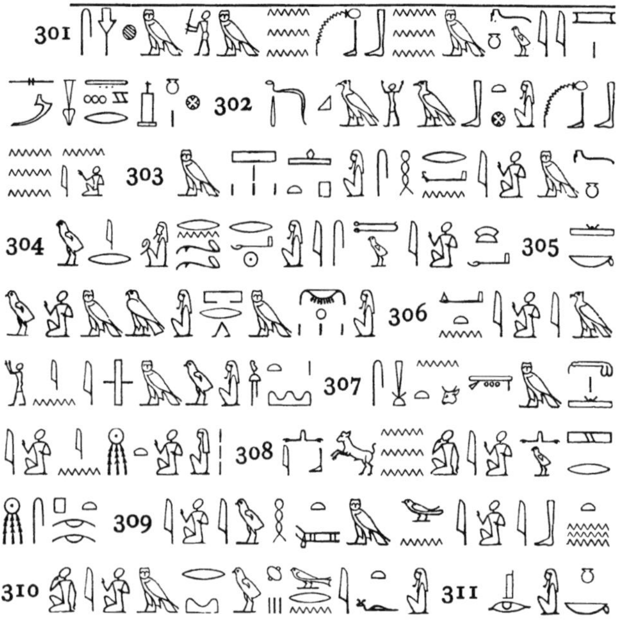

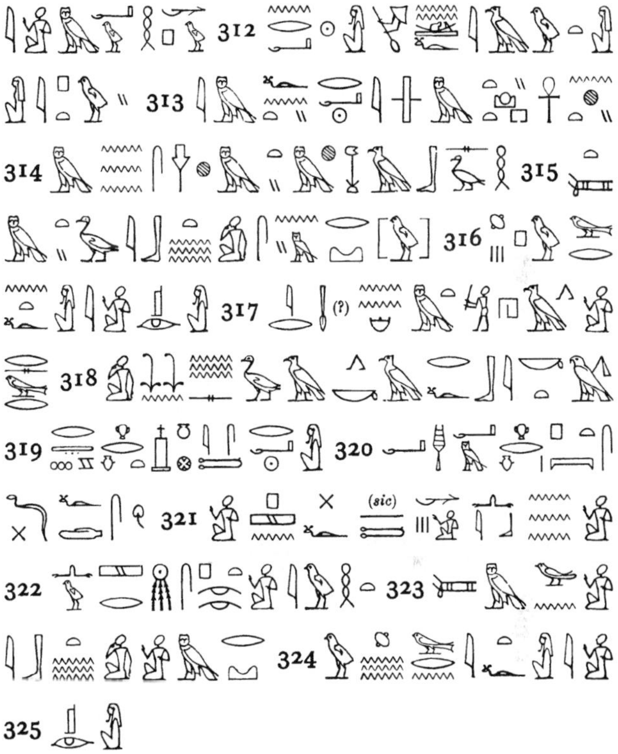

13. Of bringing a boat (Chapter XCIX).

[From the sarcophagus of Ḥer (Maspero, *Mémoires*, t. I, p. 163 ff.).]

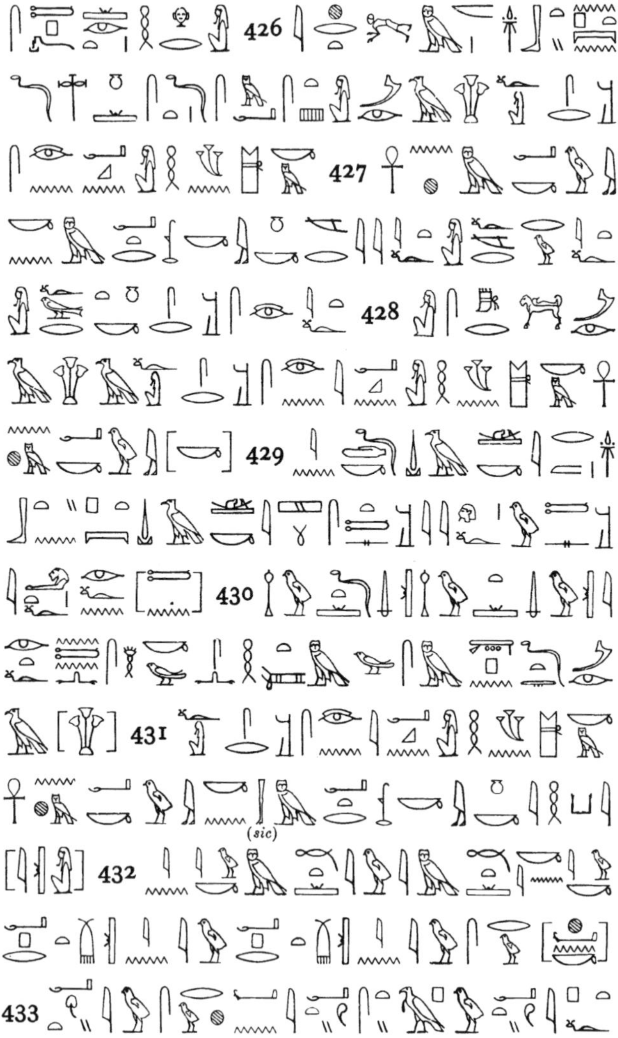
426
427
428
429
430
431
(sic)
432
433

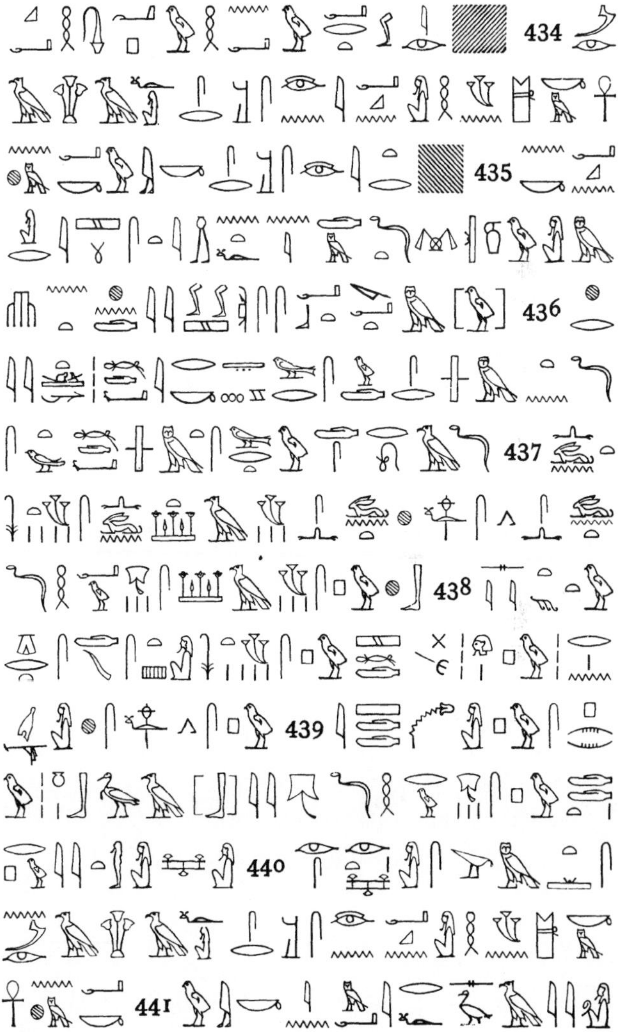
434
435
436
437
438
439
440
441

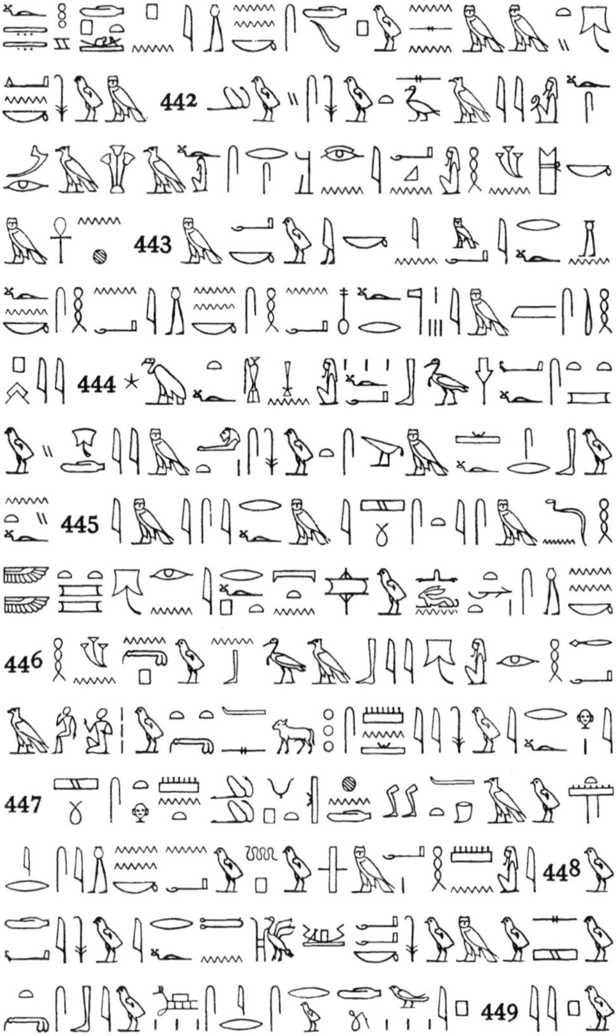
442
443
444
445
446
447
448
449

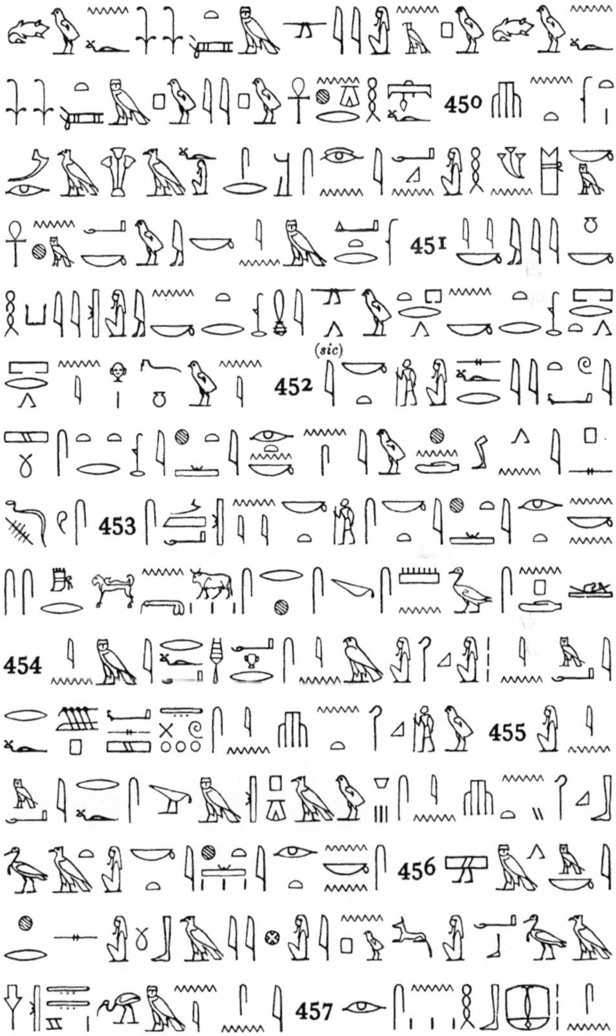
450
451
(sic)
452
453
454
455
456
457

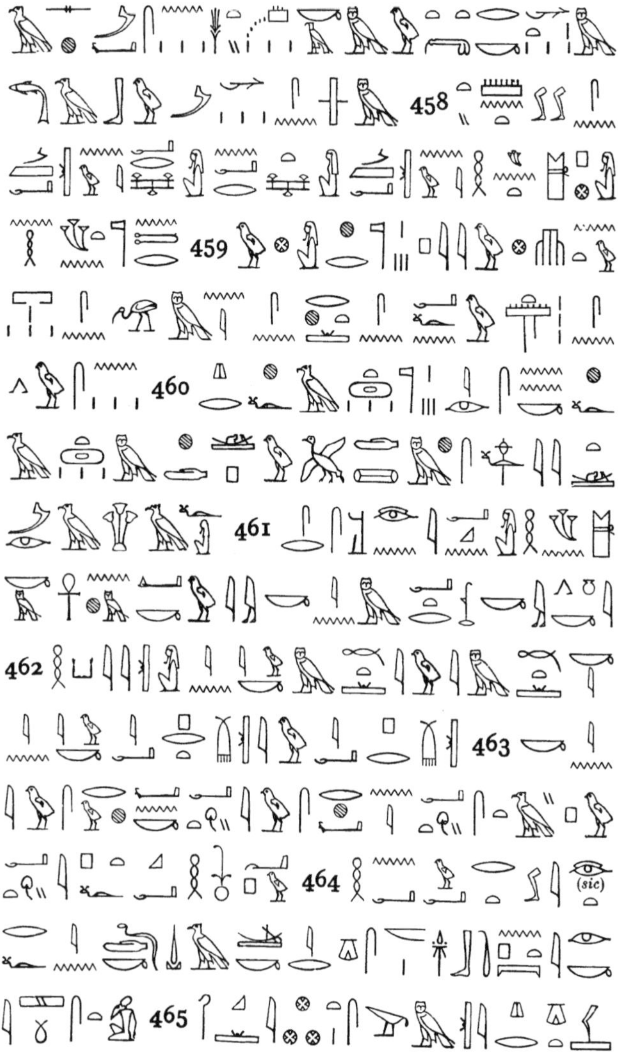
458
459
460
461
462
463
464
(sic)
465

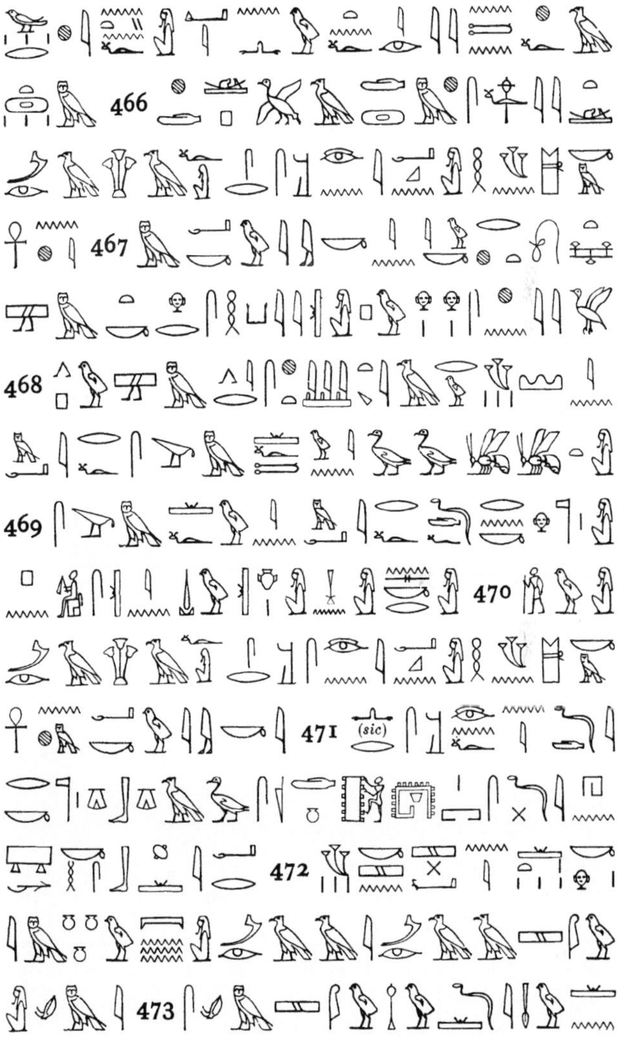
466
467
468
469
470
471
(sic)
472
473

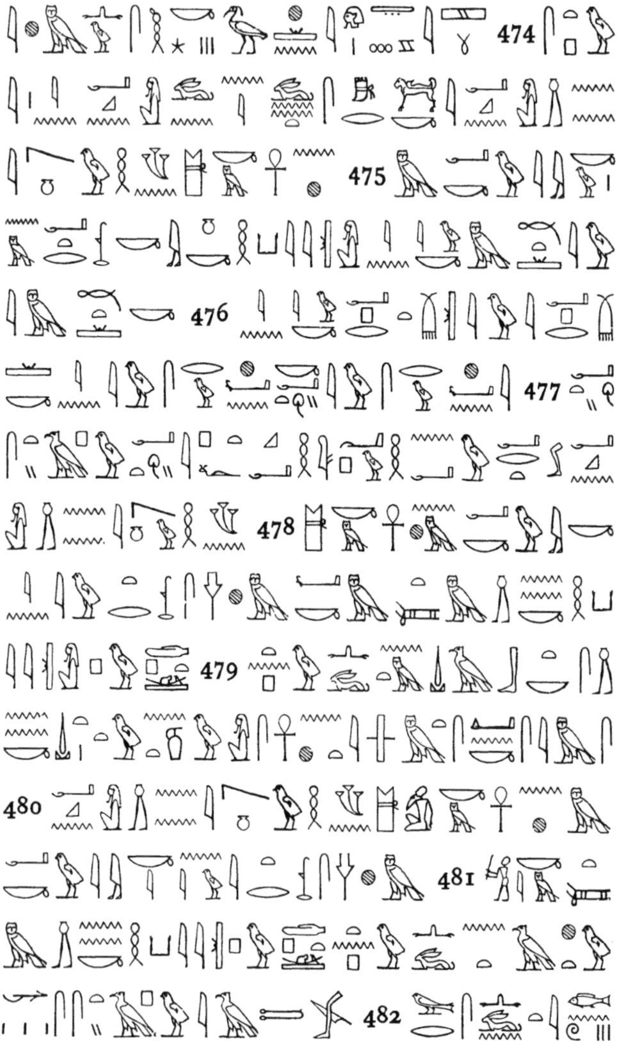
474
475
476
477
478
479
480
481
482

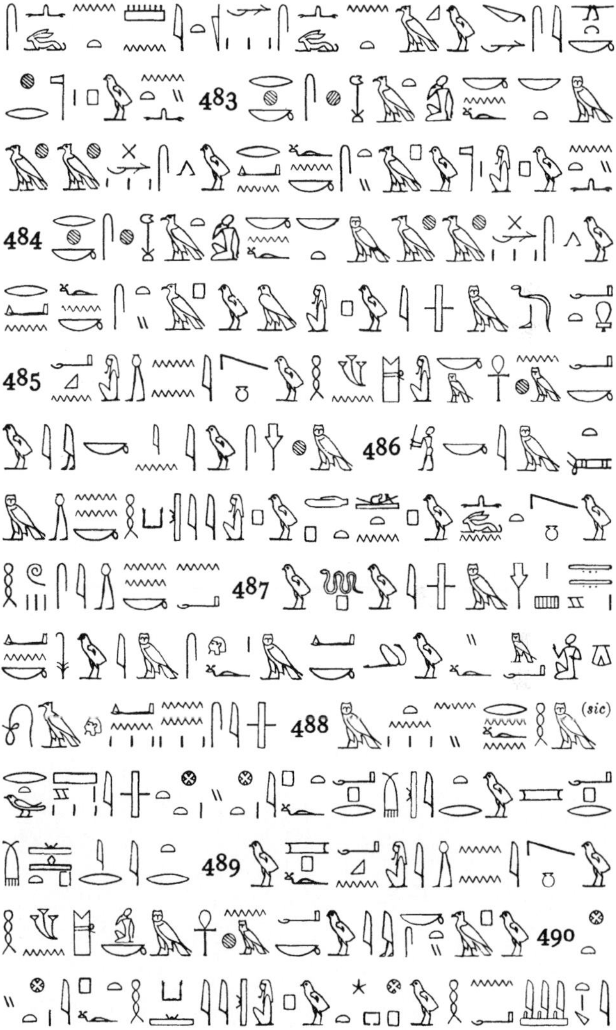
483
484
485
486
487
488
(sic)
489
490

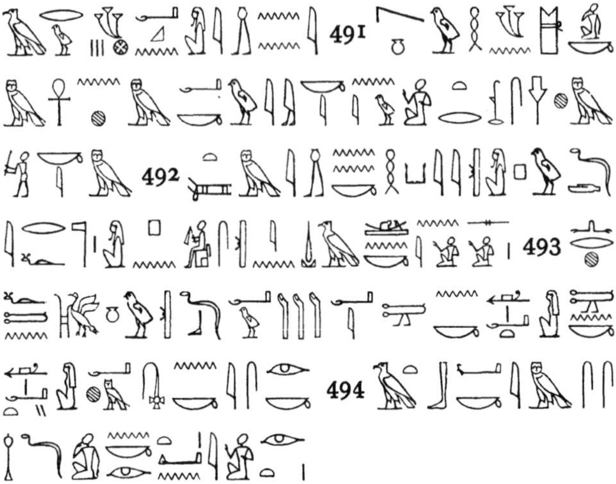

14. Of finding the Reḥti goddessess.

15. Of not being tripped up in the Other World.

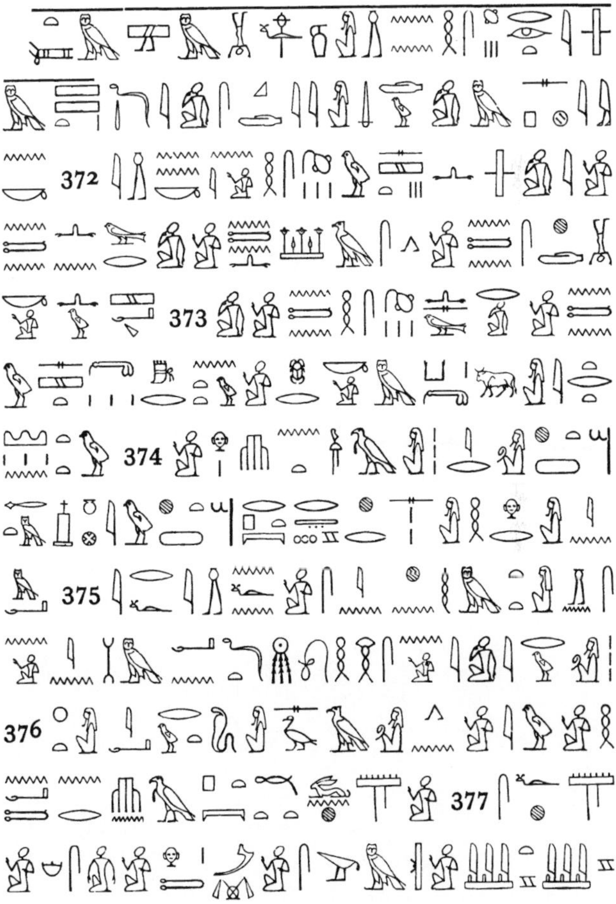

16. Of entering the Boat of Hathor.

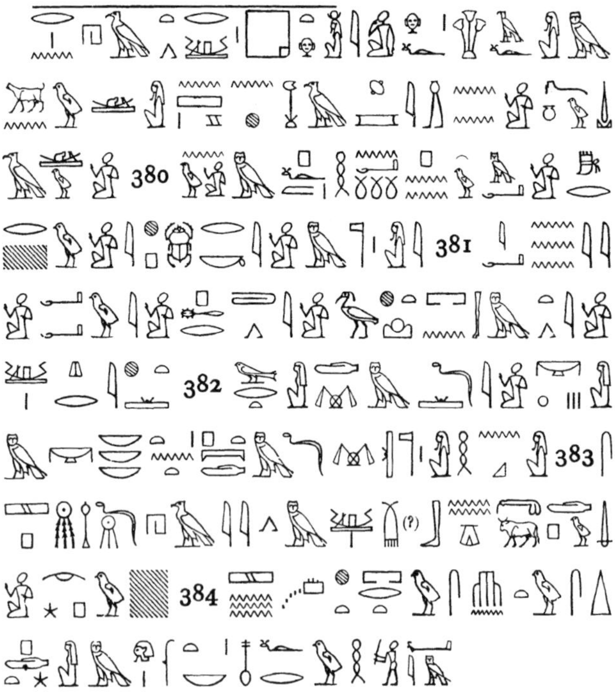

17. Of entering the Boat of Rā.

18. Of remembering words of power, or spells.

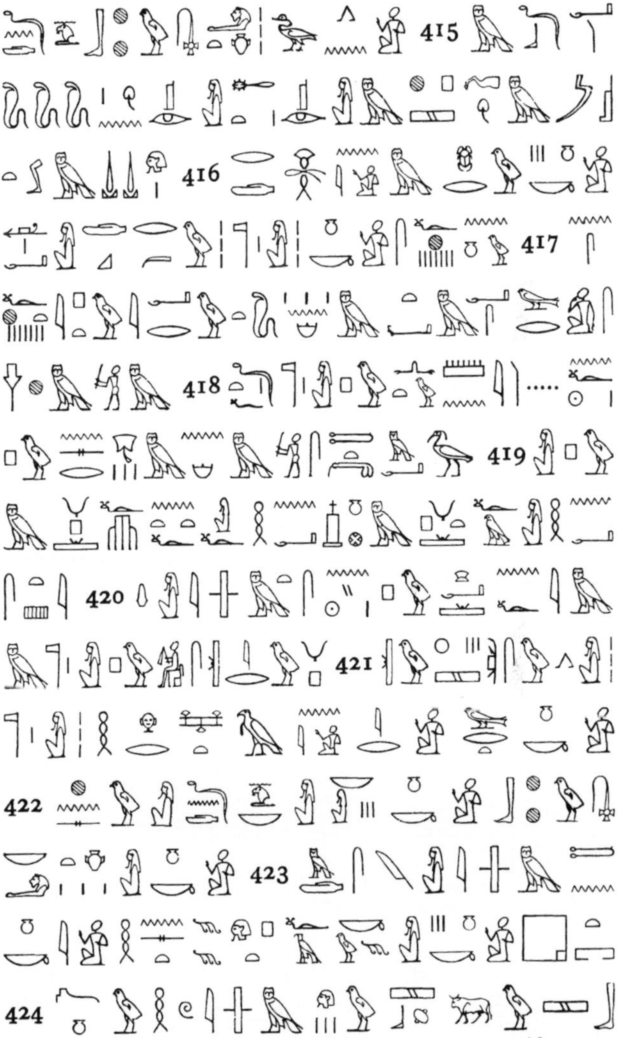
415
416
417
418
419
420
421
422
423
424

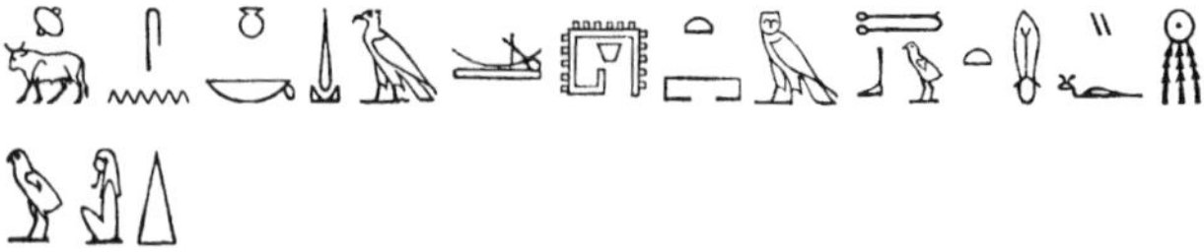

19. Of the Recognition of Friends.

From coffins in Cairo (ed. Lacau, *Recueil,* XXVI, p. 67) and the coffin of Sen in the British Museum [No. 30,839].

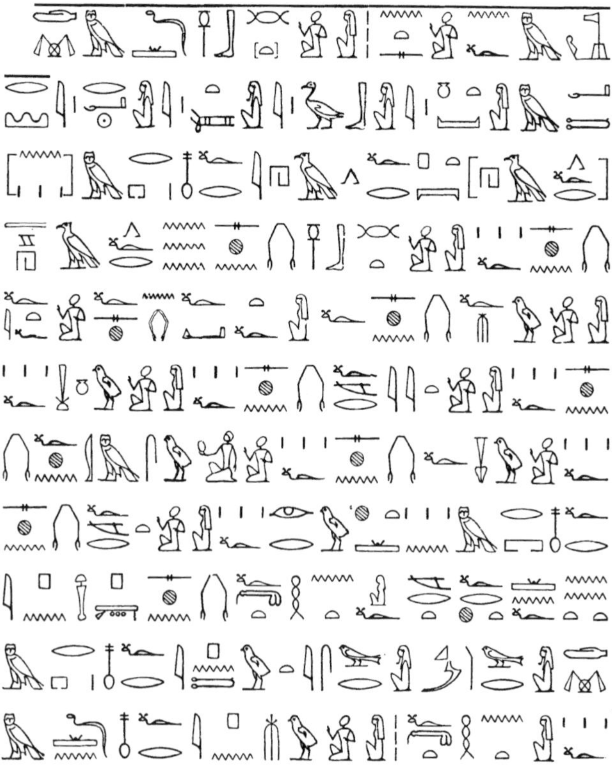

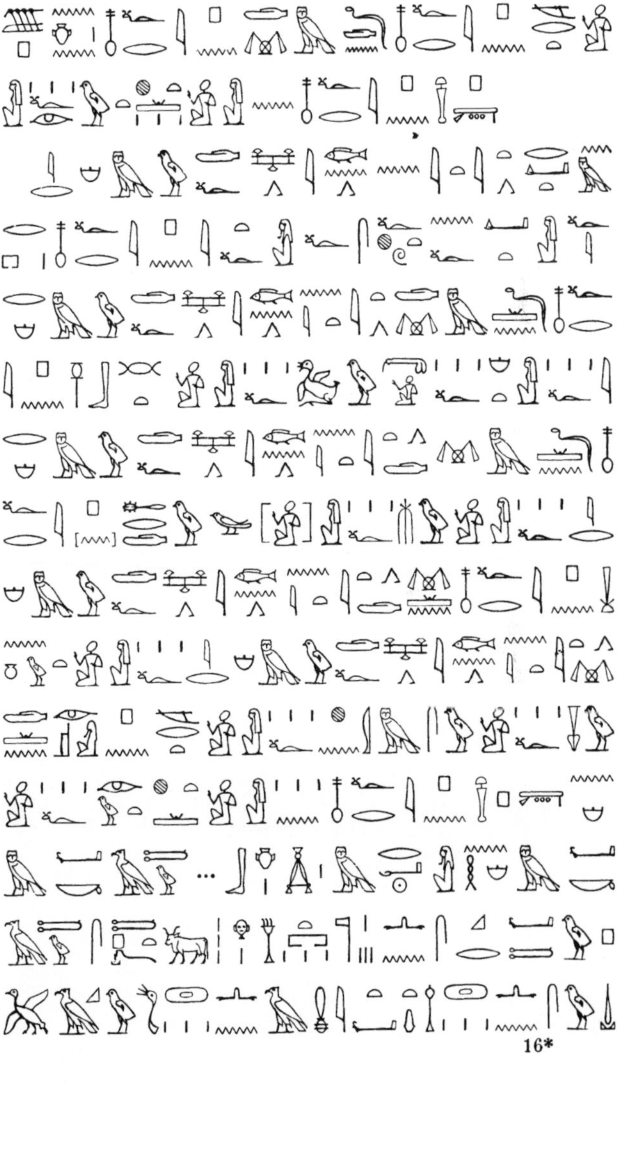

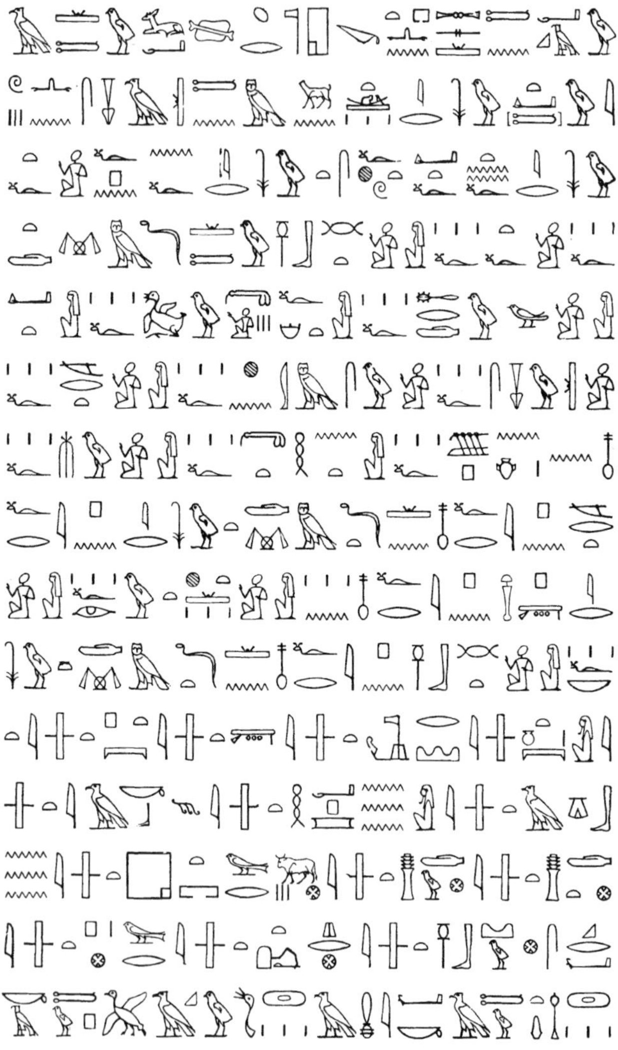

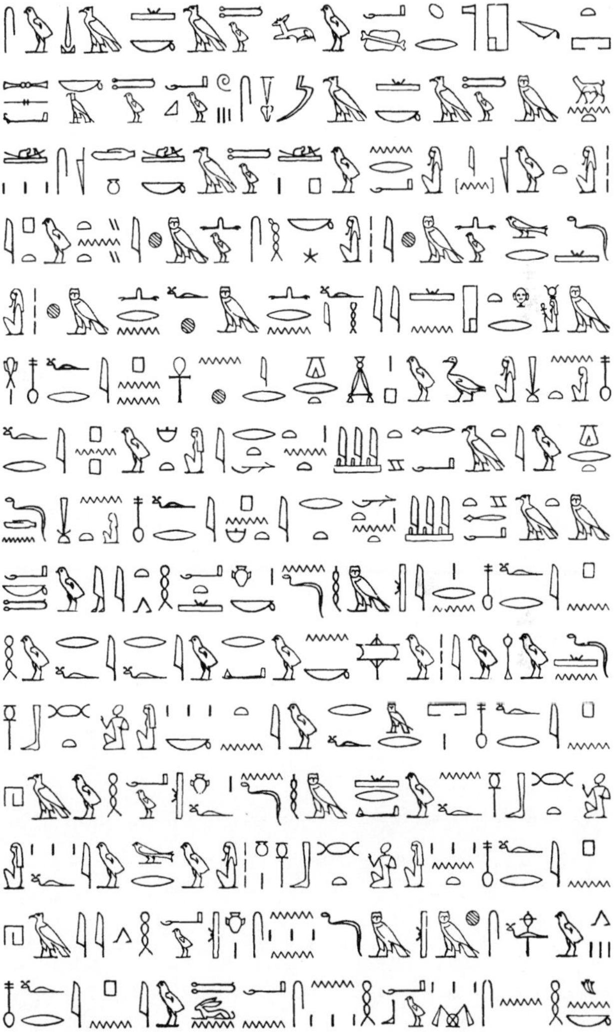

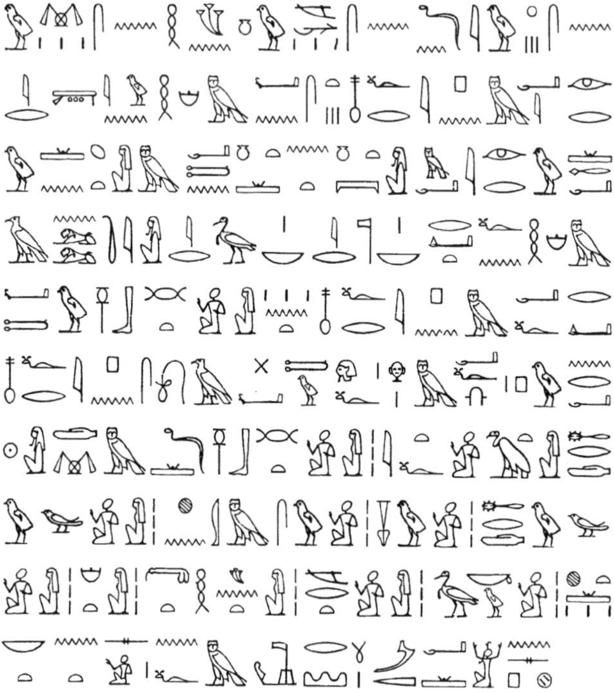

20. Of journeying in peace in the House of Osiris.

(From Schack-Schackenburg, *Buch von den zwei Wegen*, Chap. XV).

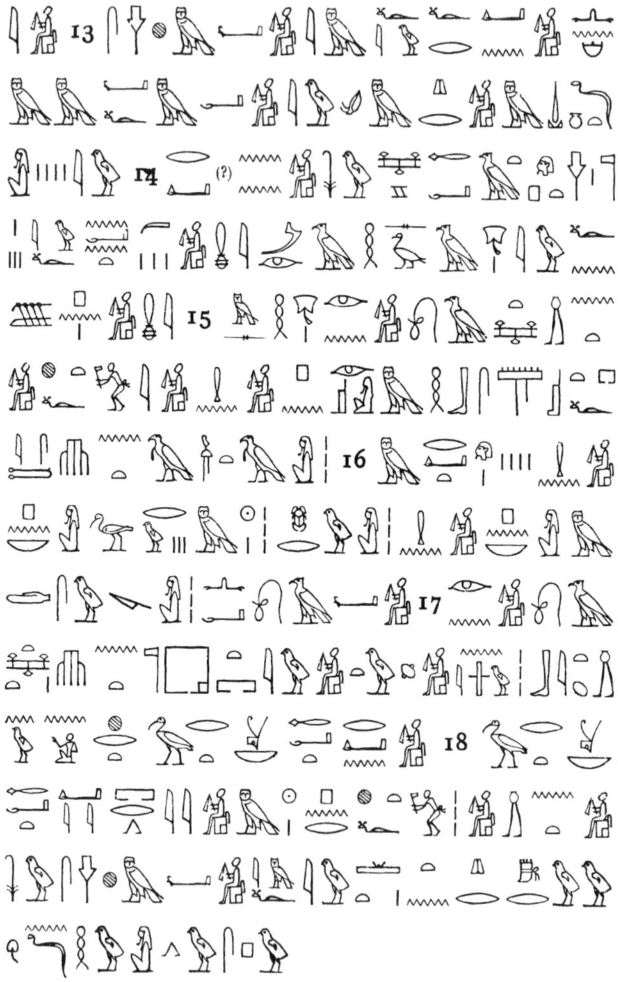
13
14
(?)
15
16
17
18

A. III.

CHAPTER XXVI.

1. [From the electrotype, Brit. Mus., No. 29,553.]

The following version of this Chapter is copied from an electrotype (Brit. Mus., No. 29,553), made from the original inscribed stone which formerly belonged to the Empress Catherine of Russia. It was accidentally discovered in the Imperial Collection of Antiquities, by the Emperor Nicholas, and was by him presented to General Peroffsky, one of his high officials. An impression was taken from the stone by Mr. Khanikoff, and was presented by Mr. Stevens to the Hon. C. A. Murray, British Minister to Persia in 1856. The electrotype measures $6^{7}/_{8}$ inches by 6 inches.

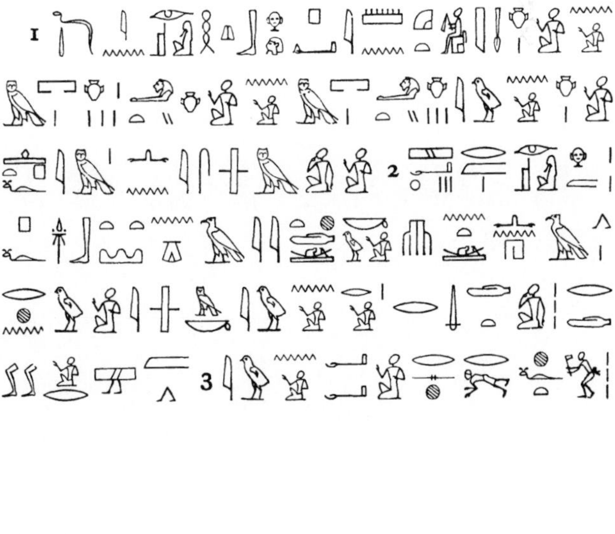

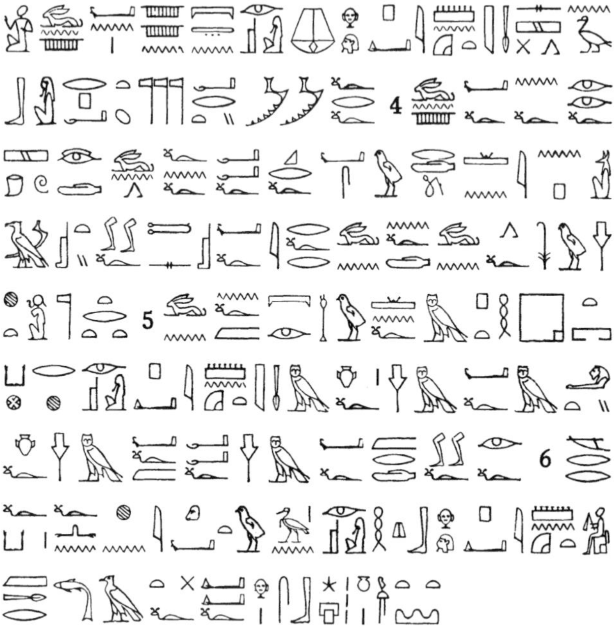

Chapter XXX B.

2. [From the electrotype, Brit. Mus., No. 29,553.]

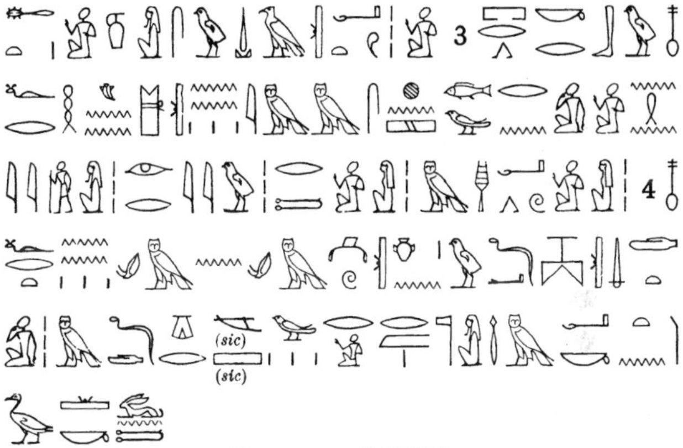

Chapter LXIV.

3. [From the electrotype, Brit. Mus., No. 29,553.]

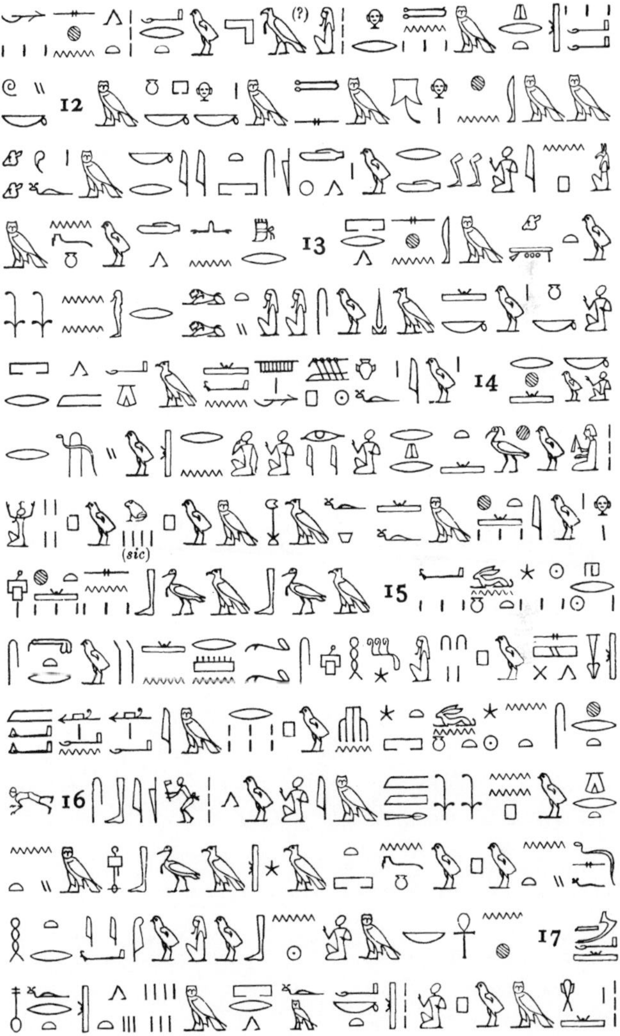
(?)
12
13
14
(sic)
15
16
17

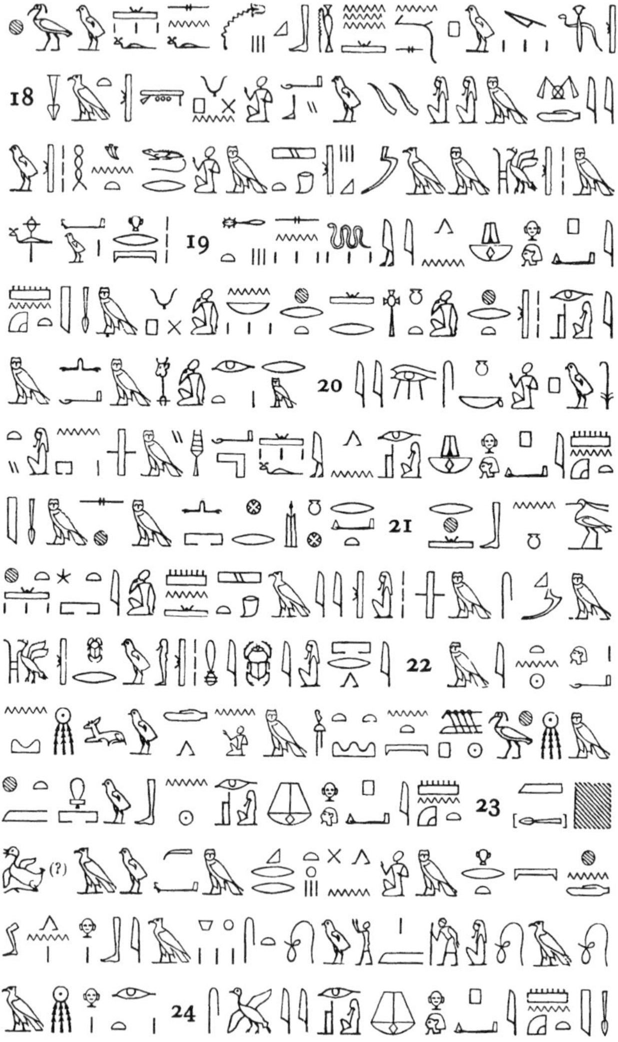
18
19
20
21
22
23
24

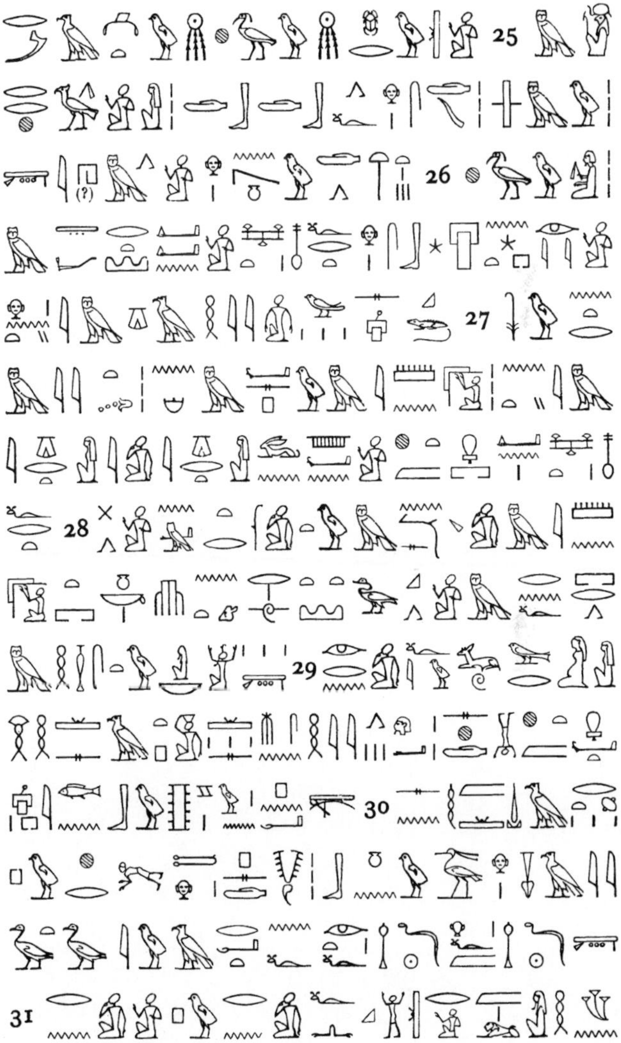
25
26
27
28
29
30
31

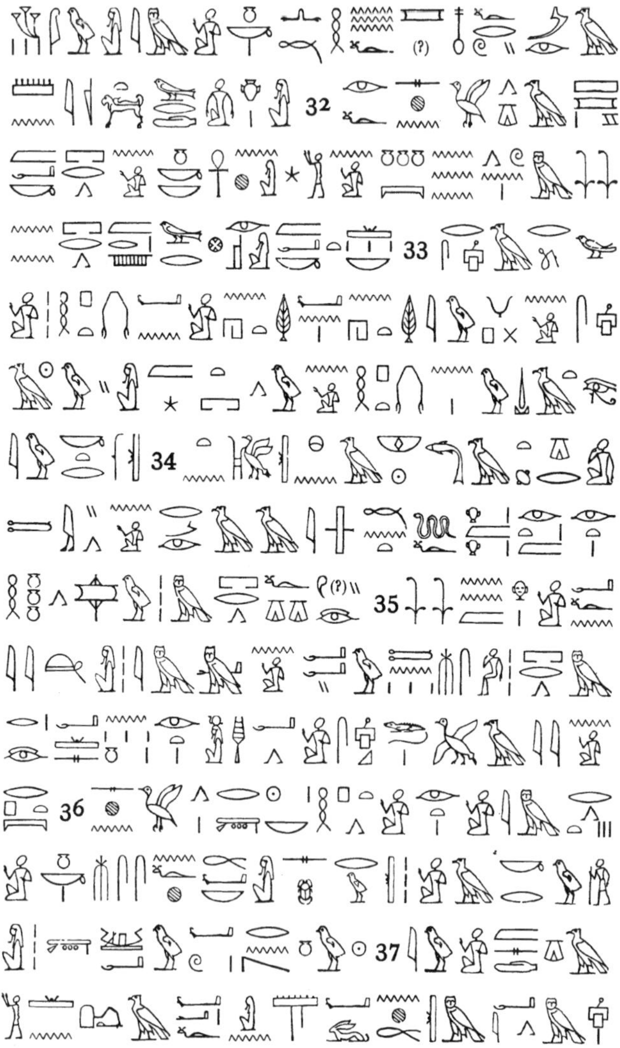
32
33
34
35
36
37

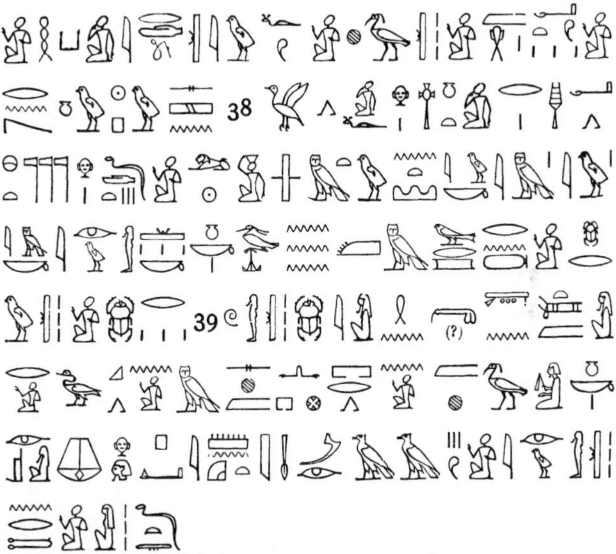

Rubric : 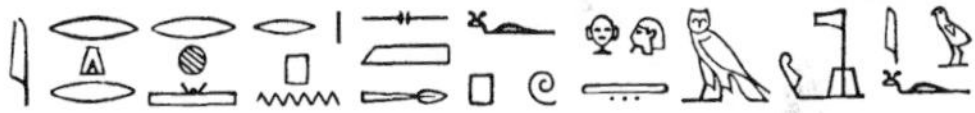

A. IV.

Chapter I.

1. [From the Coffin of Basa-en-Mut (Brit. Mus., No. 22,940).]

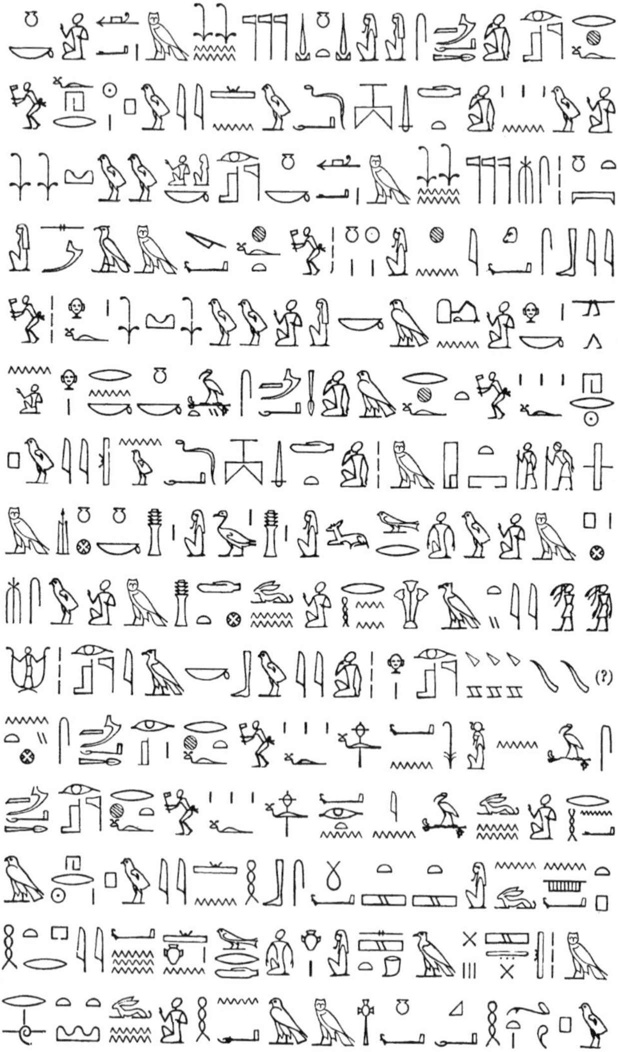

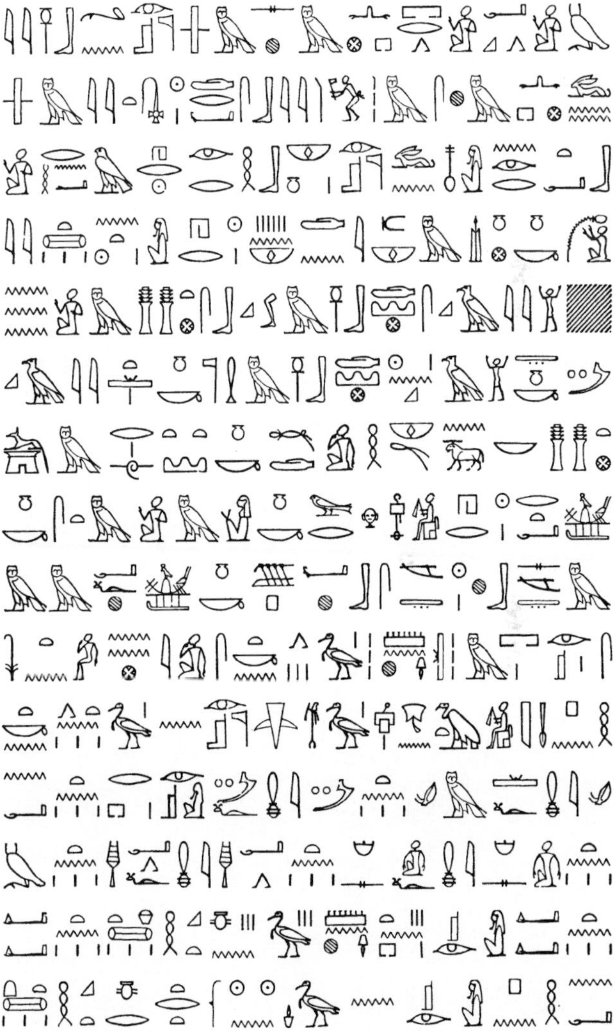

CHAPTER II.

2. [From the Coffin of Basa-en-Mut (Brit. Mus., No. 22,940).]

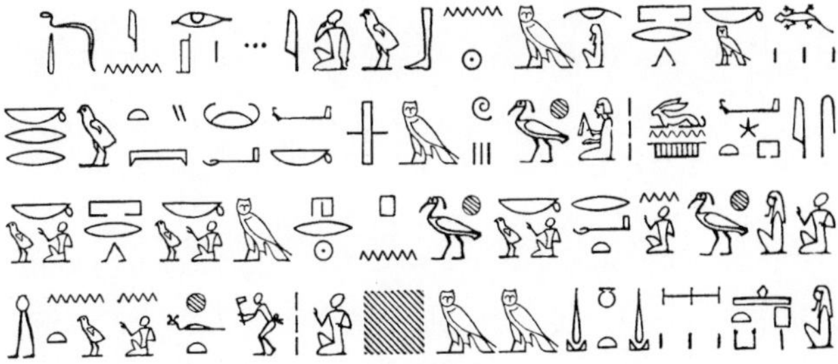

Chapter IX.

3. [From the Coffin of Basa-en-Mut (Brit. Mus., No. 22,940).]

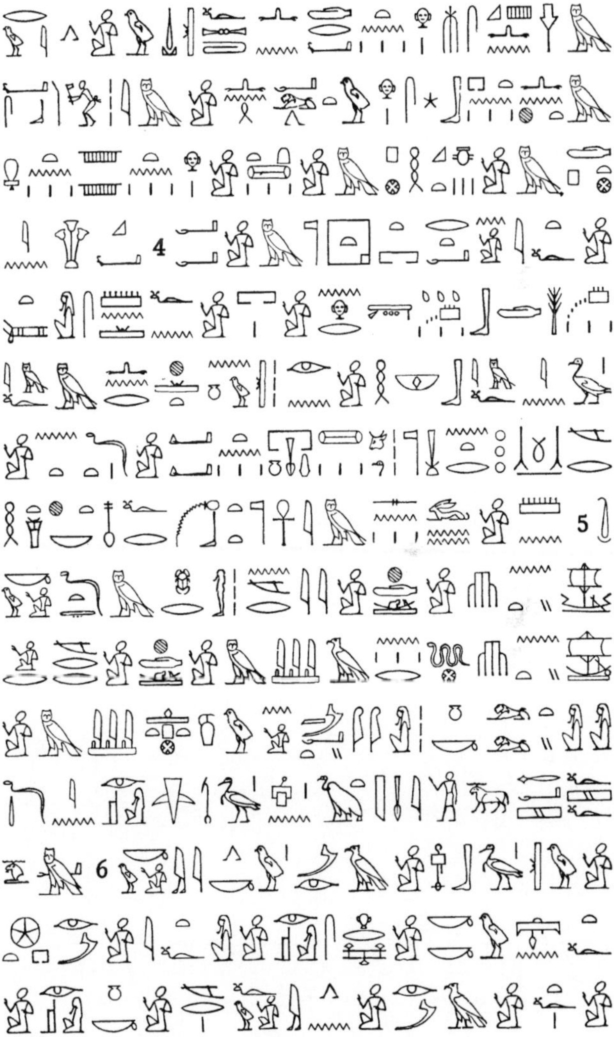

Chapter X.

4. [From the Coffin of Basa-en-Mut (Brit. Mus., No. 22,940).]

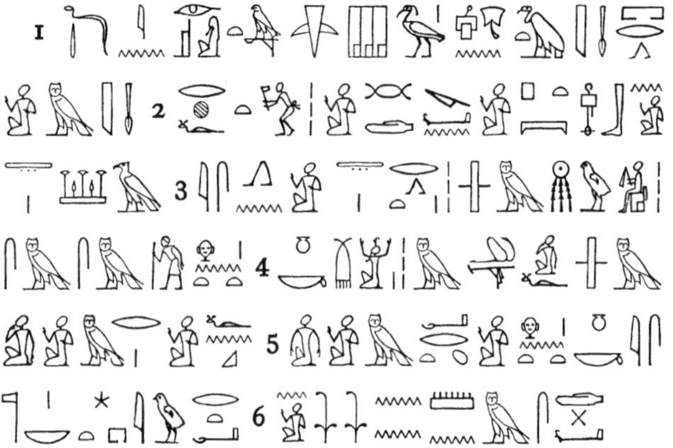

CHAPTER XXIII.

5. [From the Coffin of Basa-en-Mut (Brit. Mus., No. 22,940).]

CHAPTER XXIV.

6. [From the Coffin of Basa-en-Mut (Brit. Mus , No. 22,940).]

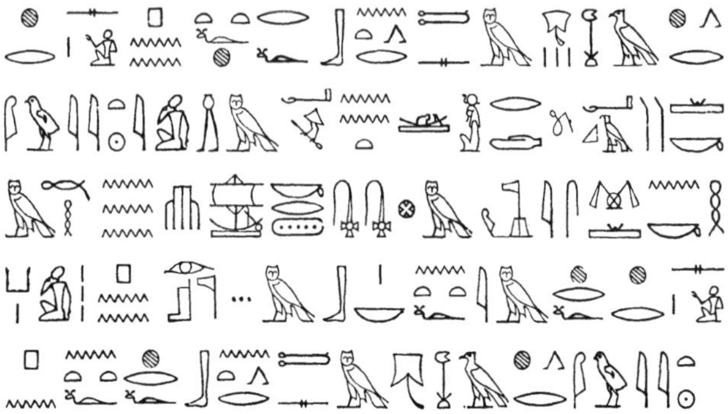

Chapter XXVI.

7. [From the Coffin of Basa-en-Mut (Brit. Mus., No. 22,940).]

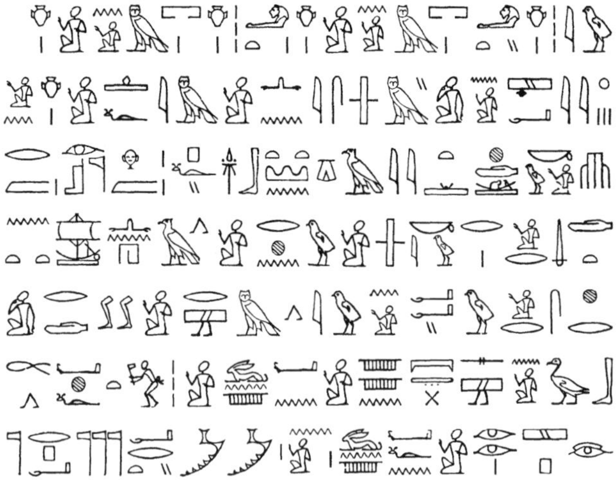

CHAPTER XXVIII.

8. [From the Coffin of Basa-en-Mut (Brit. Mus., No. 22,940).]

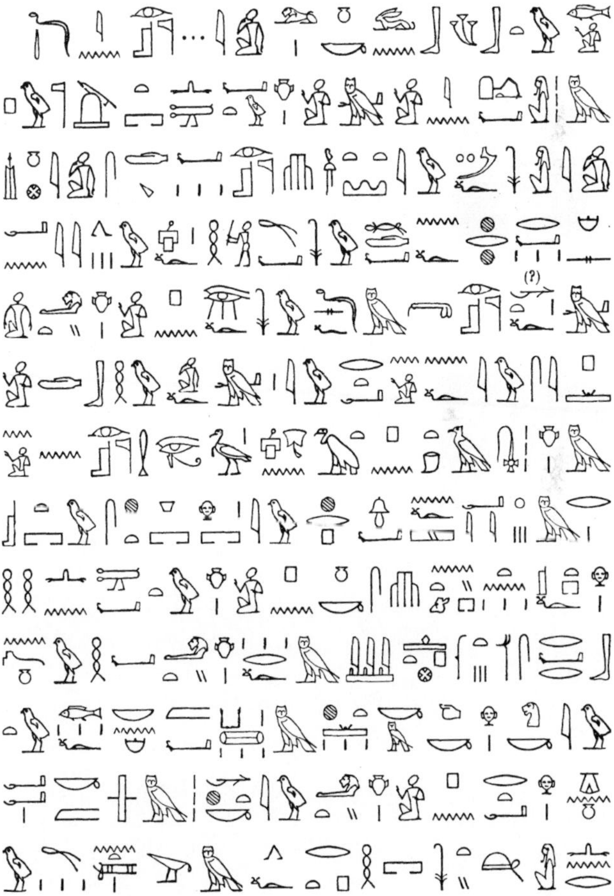

CHAPTER XXX B.

9. [From the Coffin of Basa-en-Mut (Brit. Mus., No. 22,940).]

CHAPTER XXXI.

10. [From the Coffin of Basa-en-Mut (Brit. Mus., No. 22,940).]

CHAPTER XLIV.

11. [From the Coffin of Basa-en-Mut (Brit. Mus., No. 22,940).]

CHAPTER XLVII.

12. [From the Coffin of Basa-en-Mut (Brit. Mus., No. 22,940).]

CHAPTER LVI.

13. [From the Coffin of Basa-en-Mut (Brit. Mus., No. 22,940).]

Chapter LIX.

14. [From the Coffin of Basa-en-Mut (Brit. Mus., No. 22,940).]

Chapter LXIII a.

15. [From the Coffin of Basa-en-Mut (Brit. Mus., No. 22,940).]

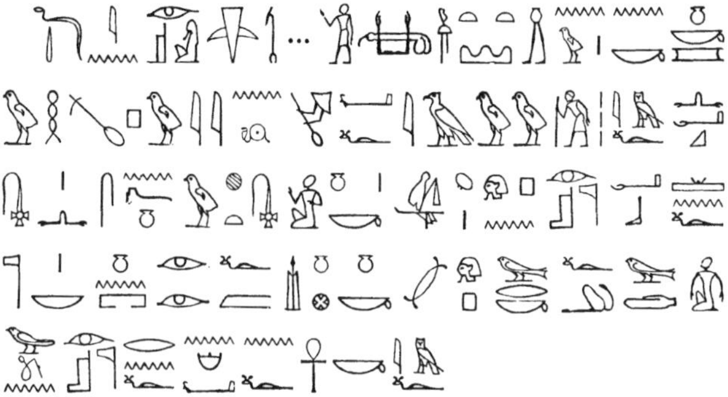

CHAPTER LXVIII.

16. [From the Coffin of Basa-en-Mut (Brit. Mus., No. 22,940).]

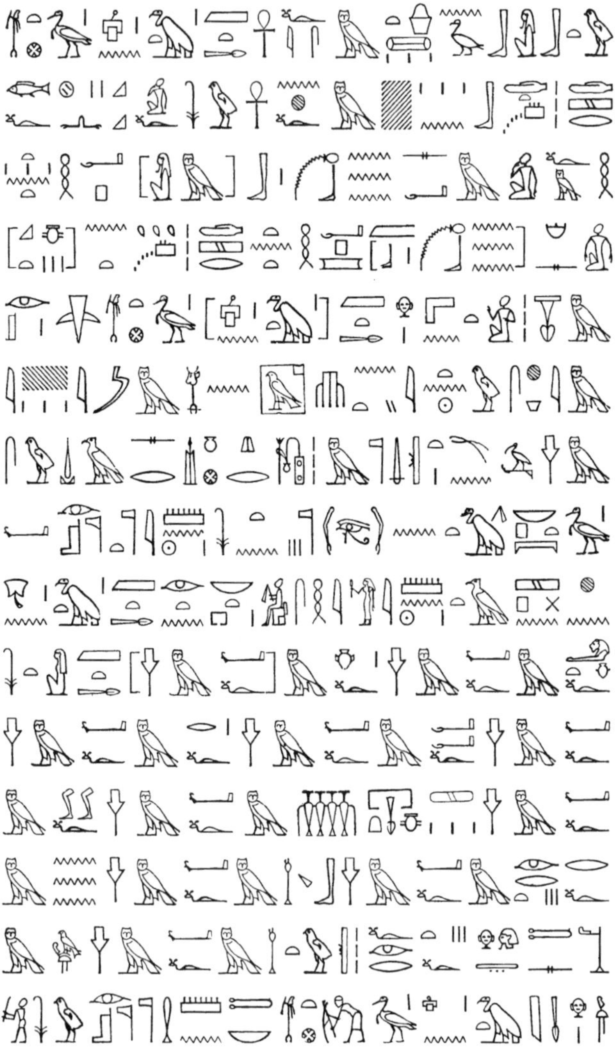

Chapter LXXI.

17. [From the Coffin of Basa-en-Mut (Brit. Mus., No. 22,940).]

Chapter LXXXIX.

18. [From the Coffin of Basa-en-Mut (Brit. Mus. No. 22,940).]

Chapter XCI.

19. [From the Coffin of Basa-en-Mut (Brit. Mus. No. 22,940).]

Chapter CV.

20. [From the Coffin of Basa-en-Mut (Brit. Mus. No. 22,940).]

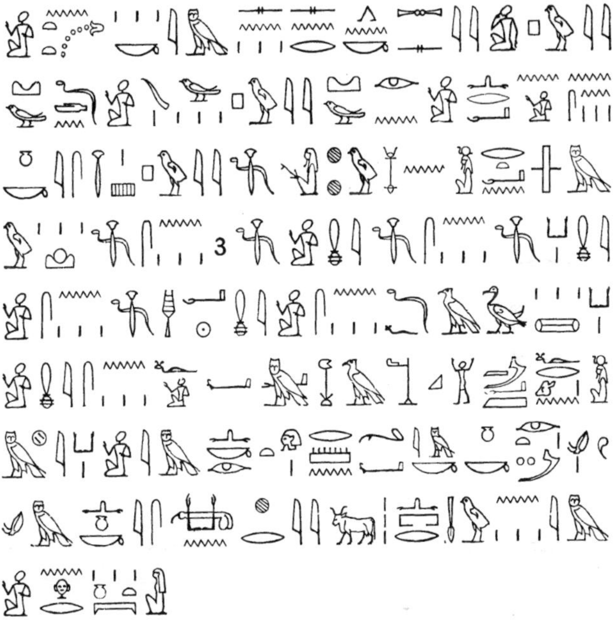

Chapter CLIV.

21. [From the Coffin of Basa-en-Mut (Brit. Mus. No. 22,940).]

ADDRESSES OF THE GODS TO BASA-EN-MUT.

22. [From the Coffin of Basa-en-Mut (Brit. Mus. No. 22,940).]

I. ḤĀPI. 

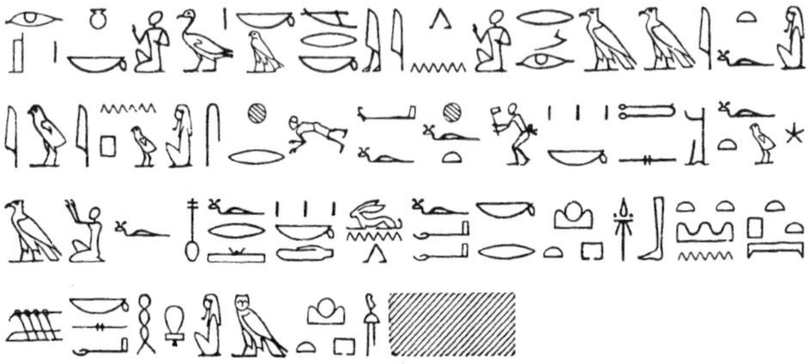

II. Defaced.

III. ȦNPU. 

IV. ḤERU-KHENT-ȦN-MERTI. 

V. Ḥaqntfȧrirenftchesef. 

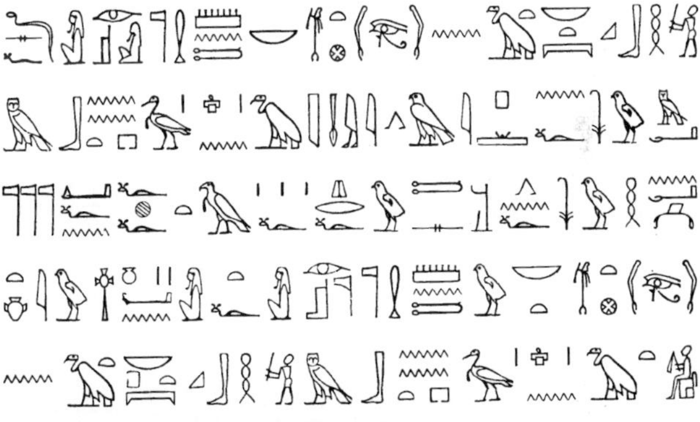

 etc.

VI. Ȧmseth. 

VII. Ṭuamutef. 

VIII. Ȧnpu. 

IX. Seb (Ḳeb). 

X. Kher-beq-f. 

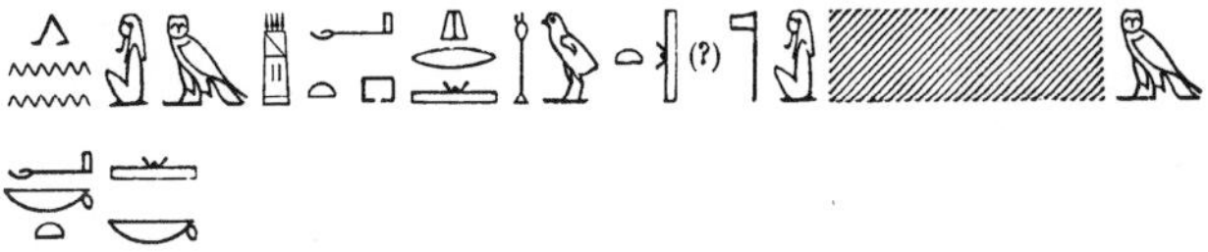

XI. [Ȧnpu]. 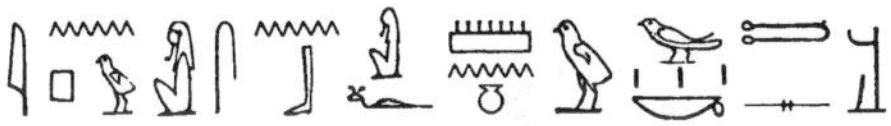

B. I.

Funerary text from the Sarcophagus of Queen Ānkhnes-nefer-ȧb-Rā (Brit. Mus. No. 811).

I. 1 

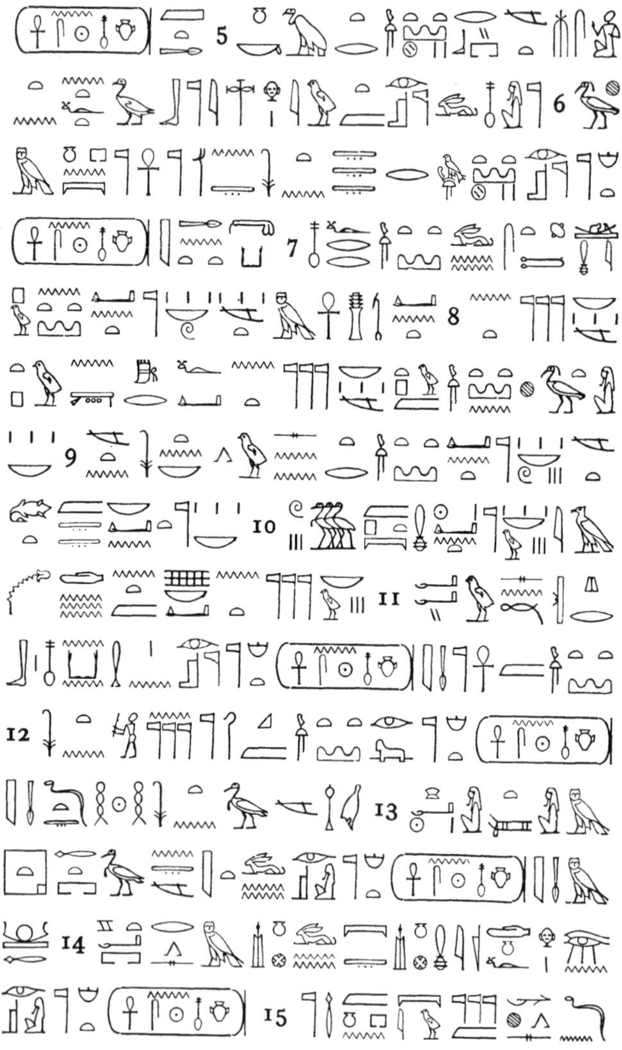

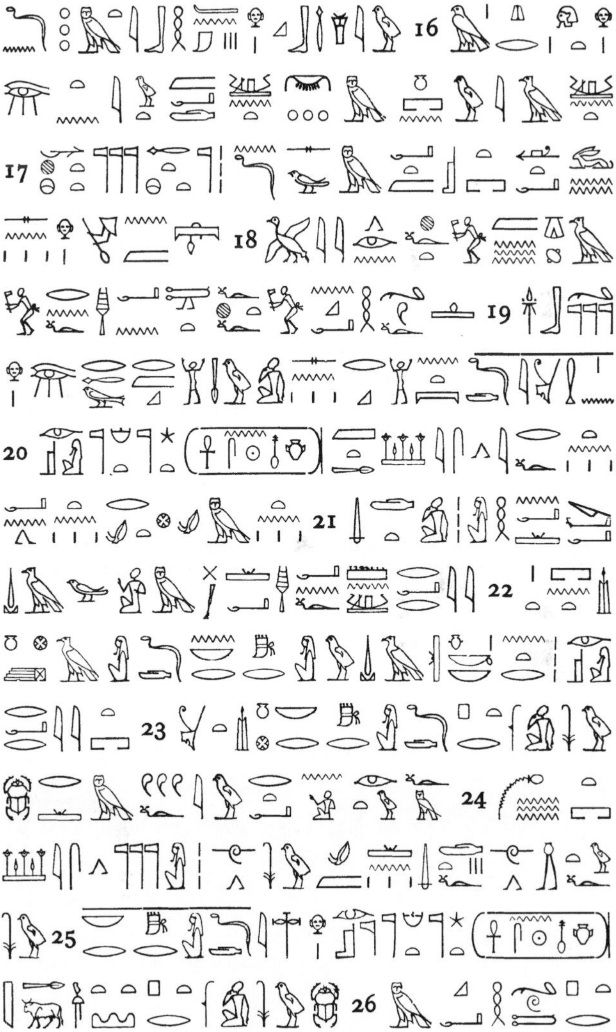

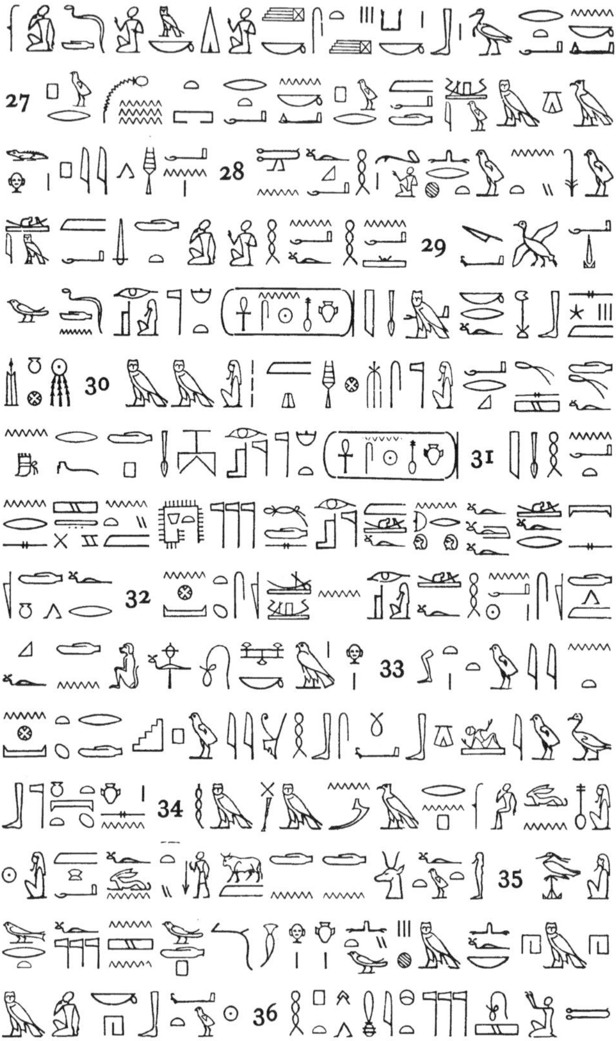

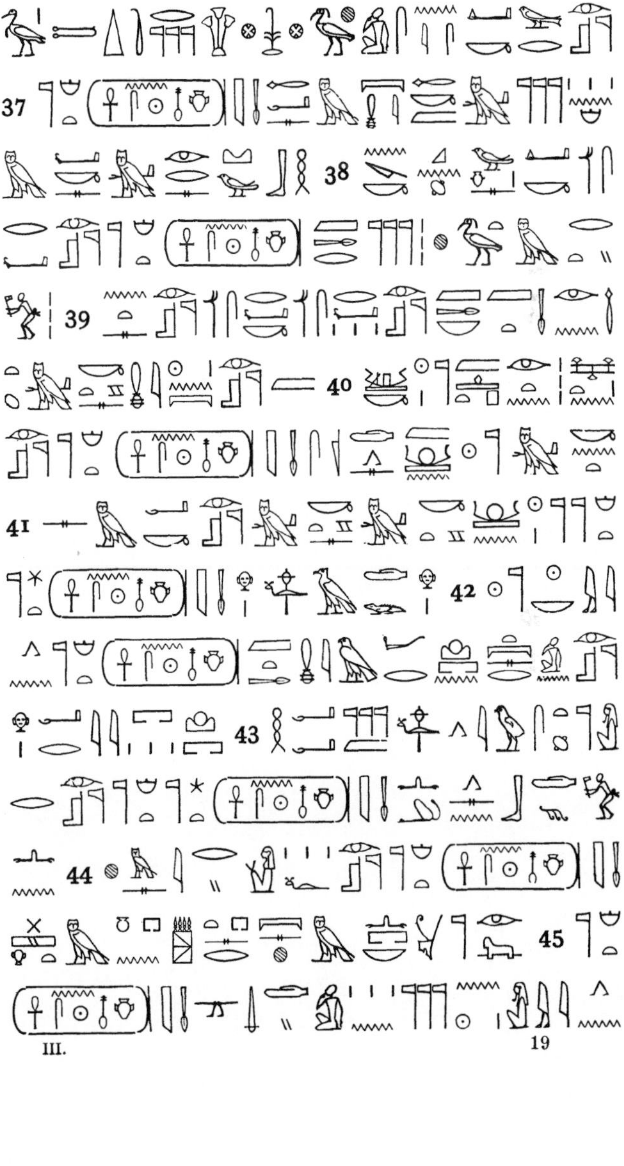

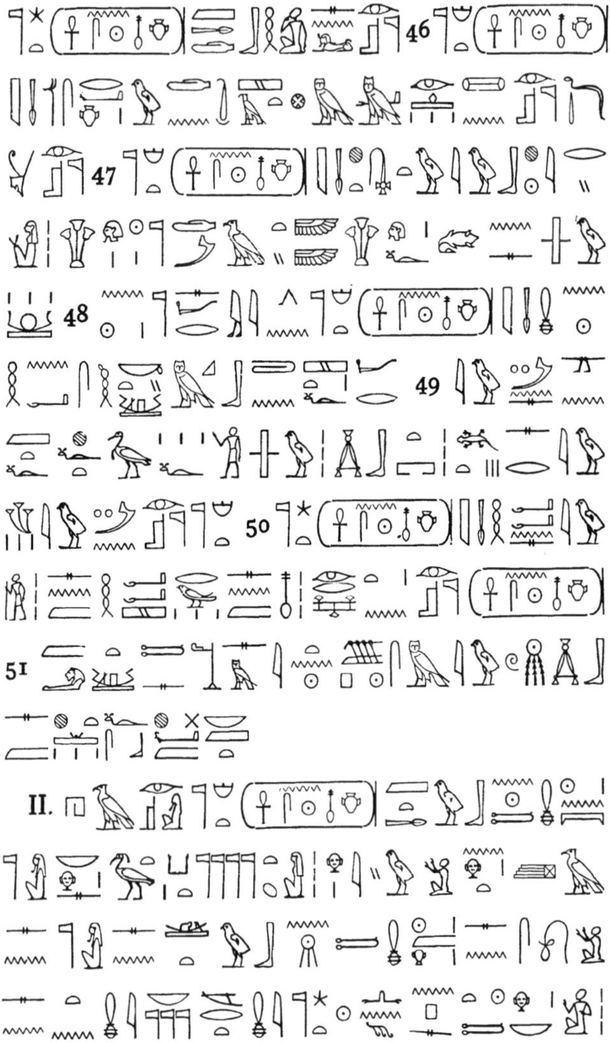
46
47
48
49
50
51
II.

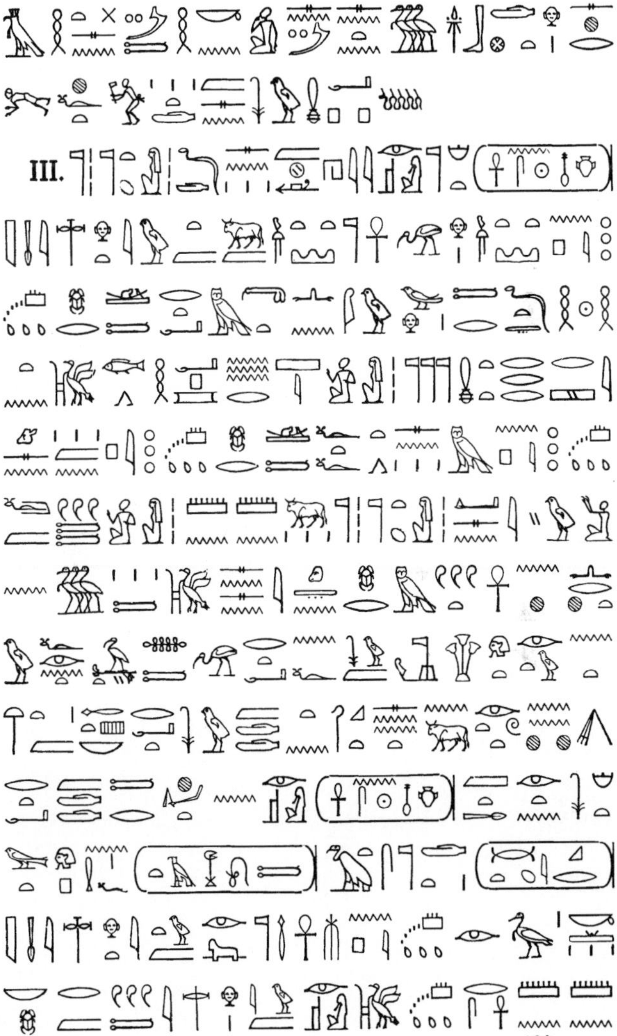

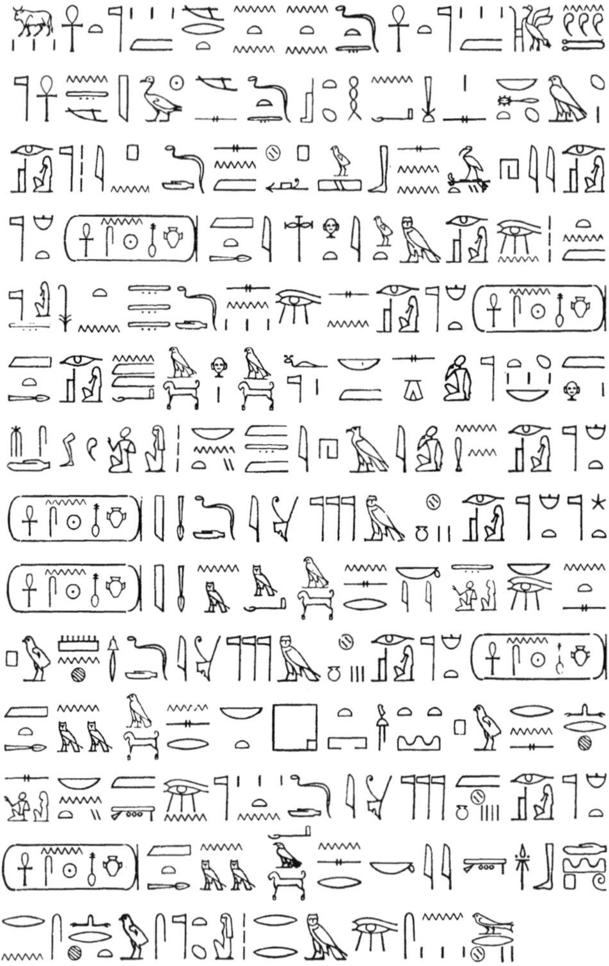

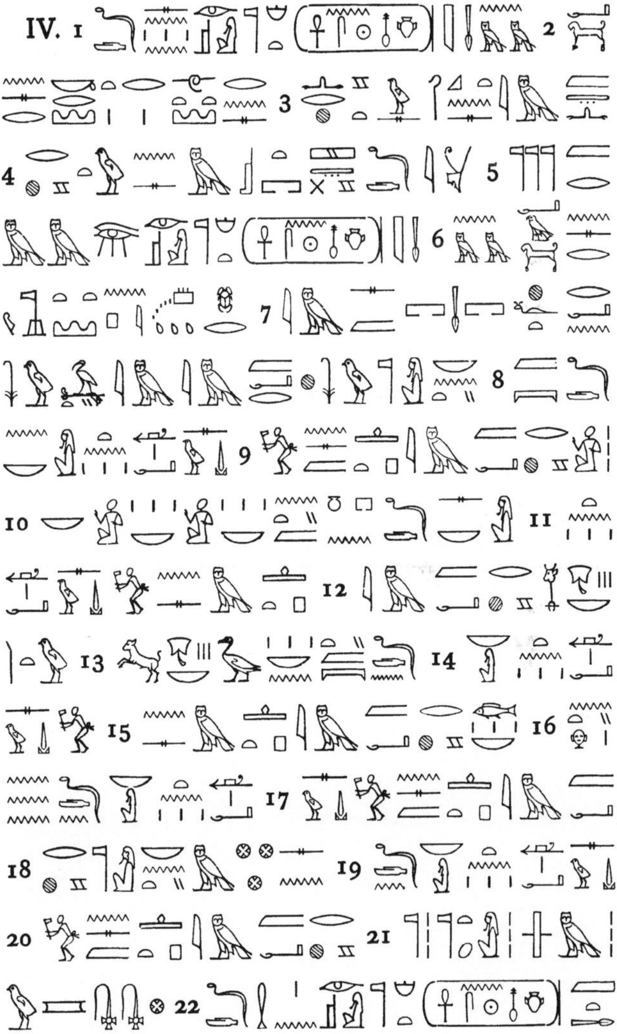

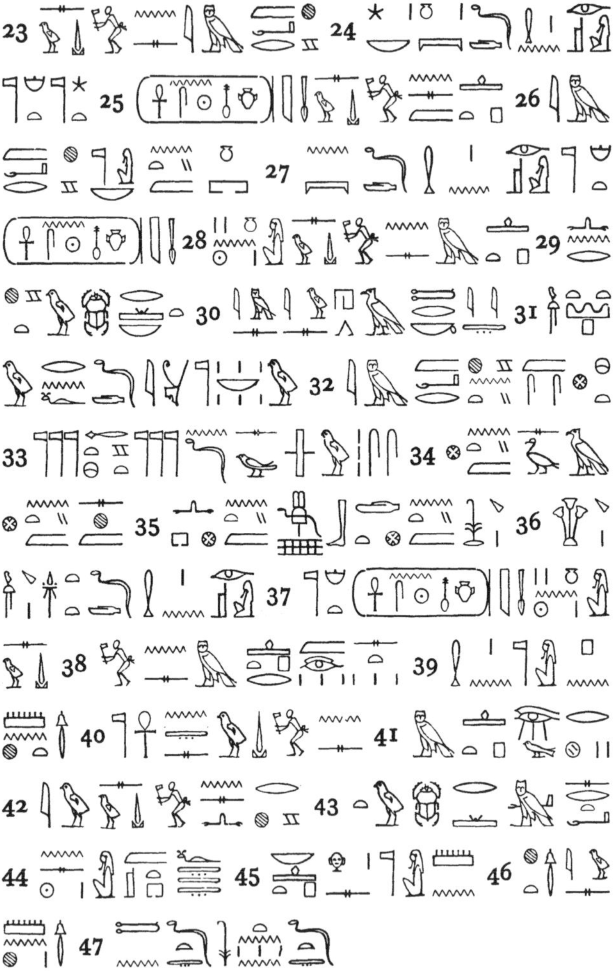
23 24
25 26
27
28 29
30 31
32
33 34
35 36
37
38 39
40 41
42 43
44 45 46
47

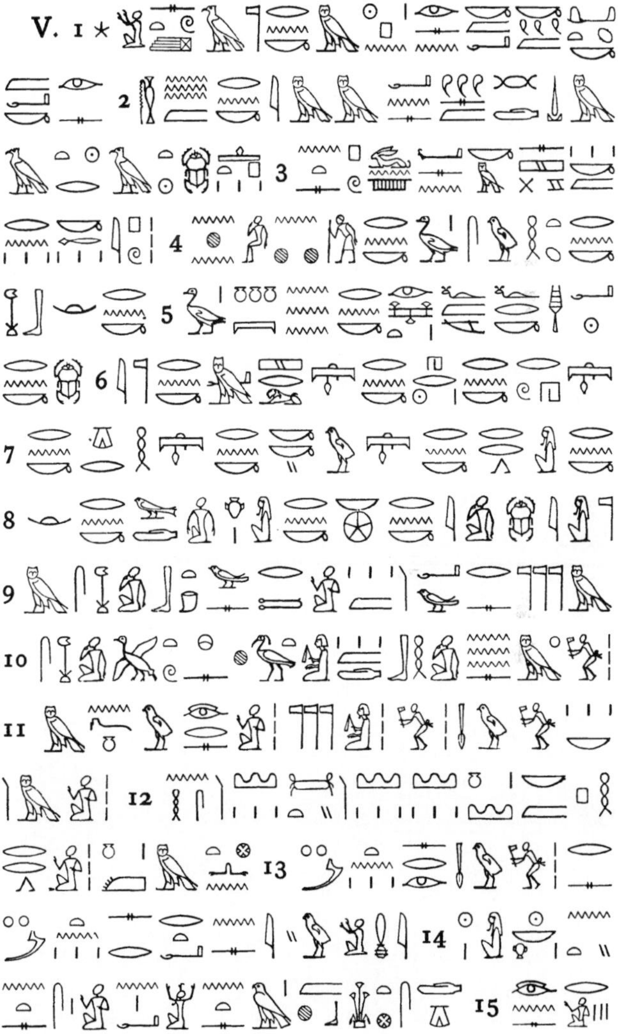

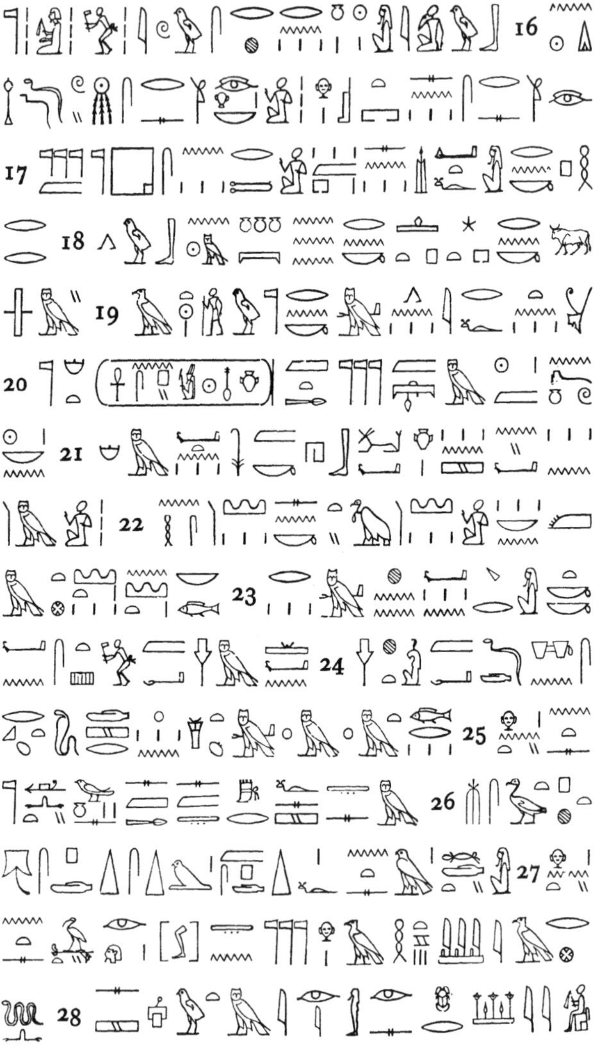

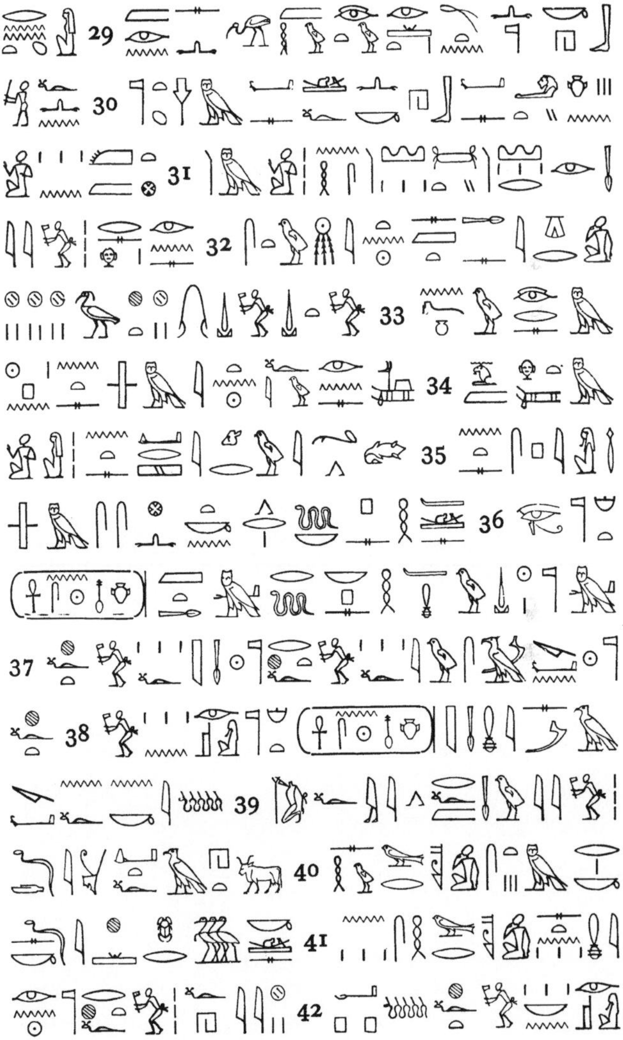

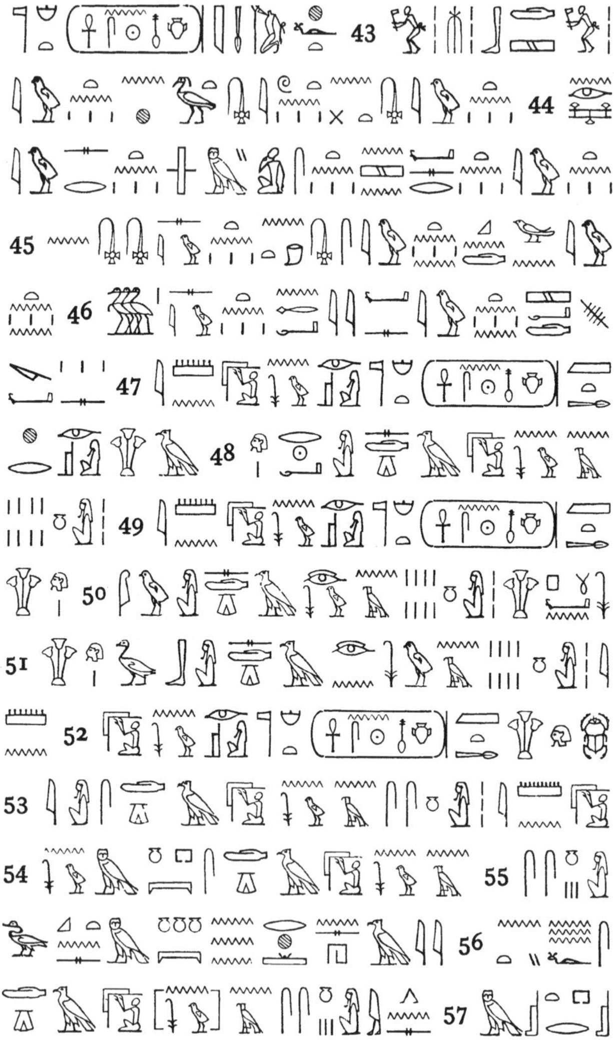

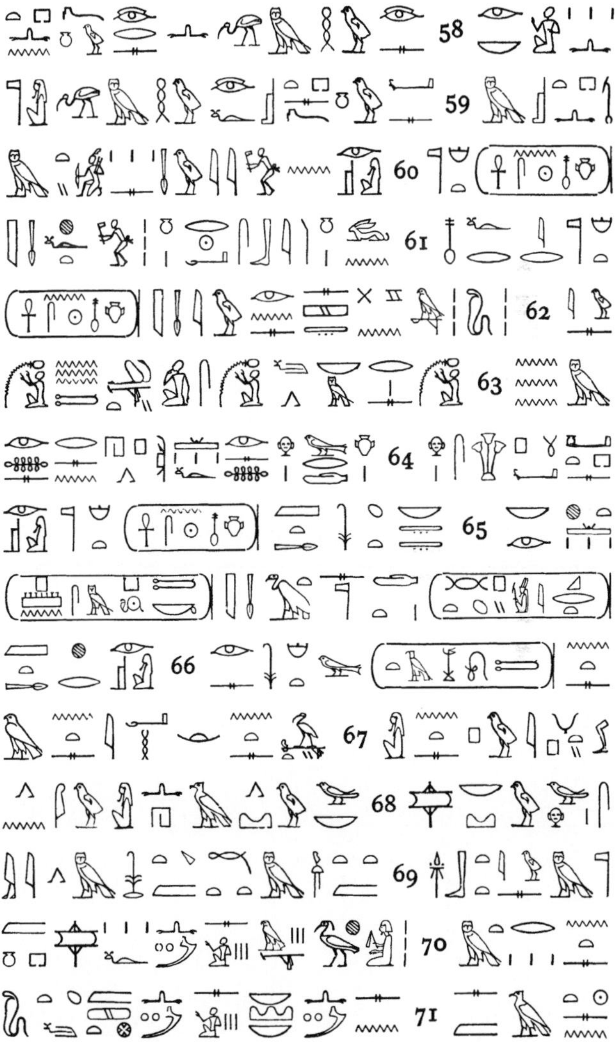
58
59
60
61
62
63
64
65
66
67
68
69
70
71

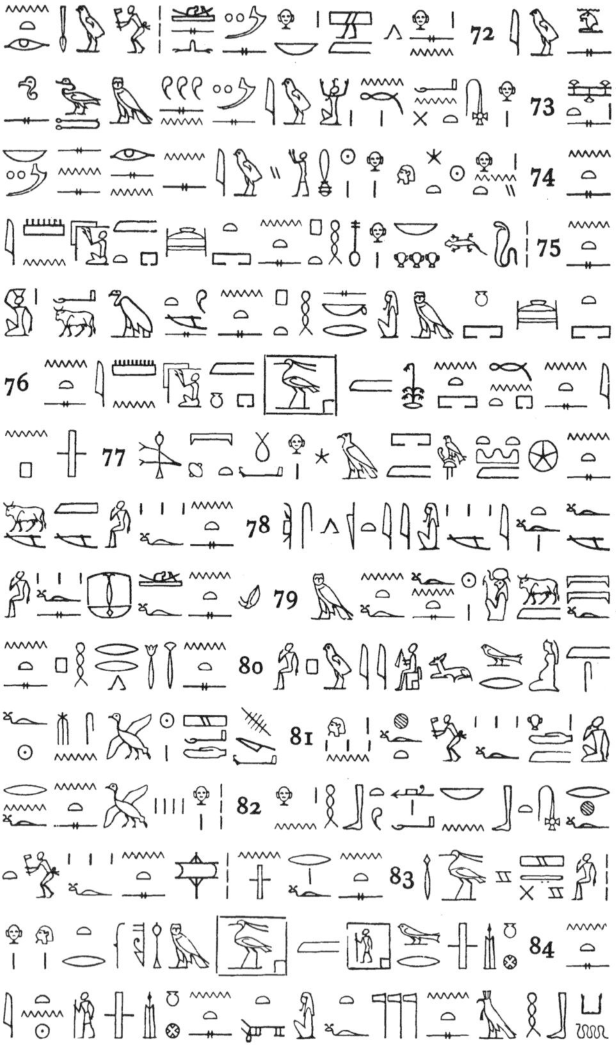
72
73
74
75
76
77
78
79
80
81
82
83
84

RELIGIOUS TEXTS FROM THE TOMB OF PETĀ-ÅMEN-ÅP.

(Duemichen, *Grabpalast*, II, Plate XVI; Pyramid of Unås, l. 206 ff.)

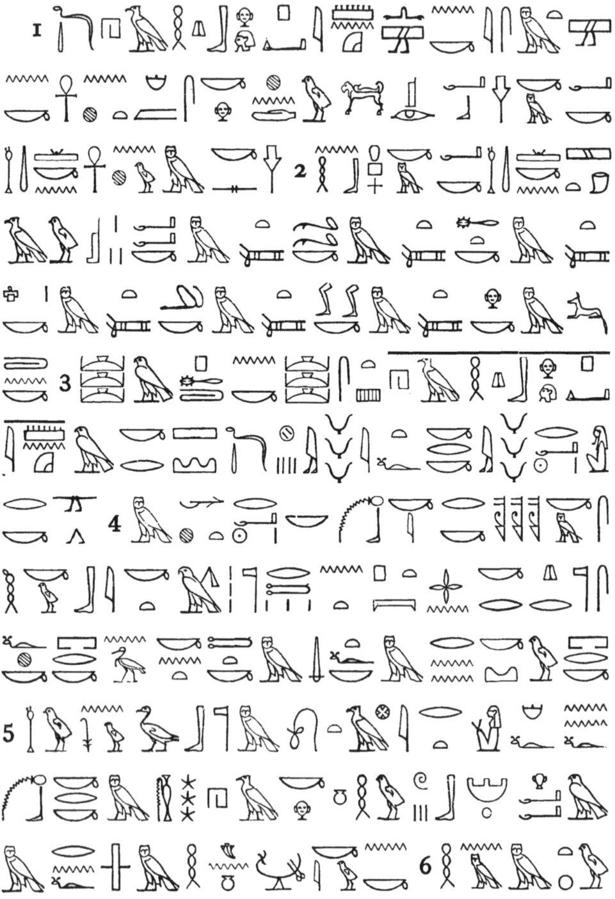

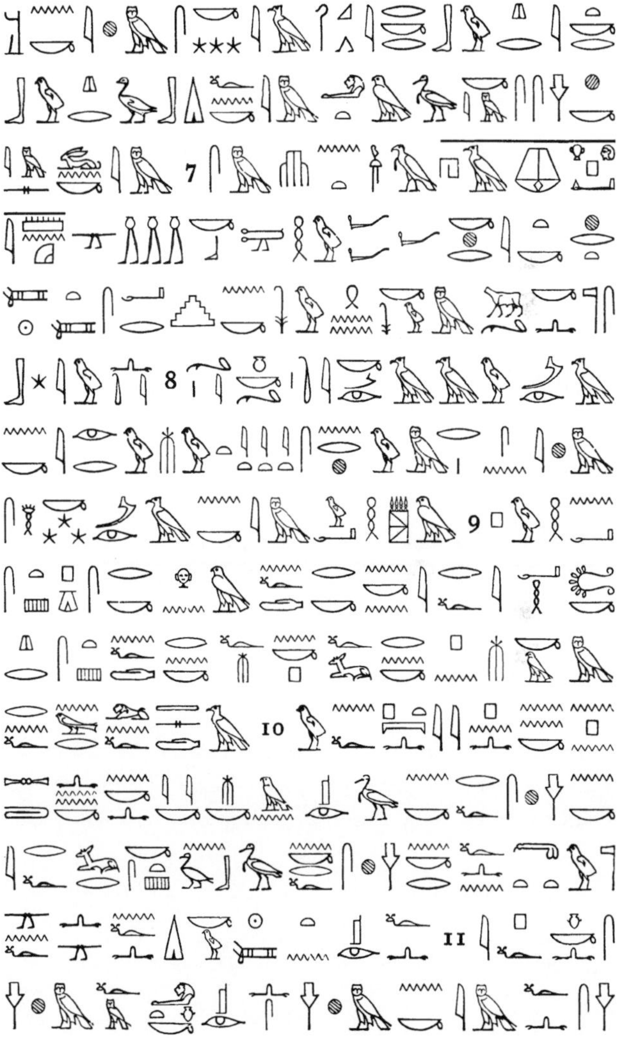
7
8
9
10
11

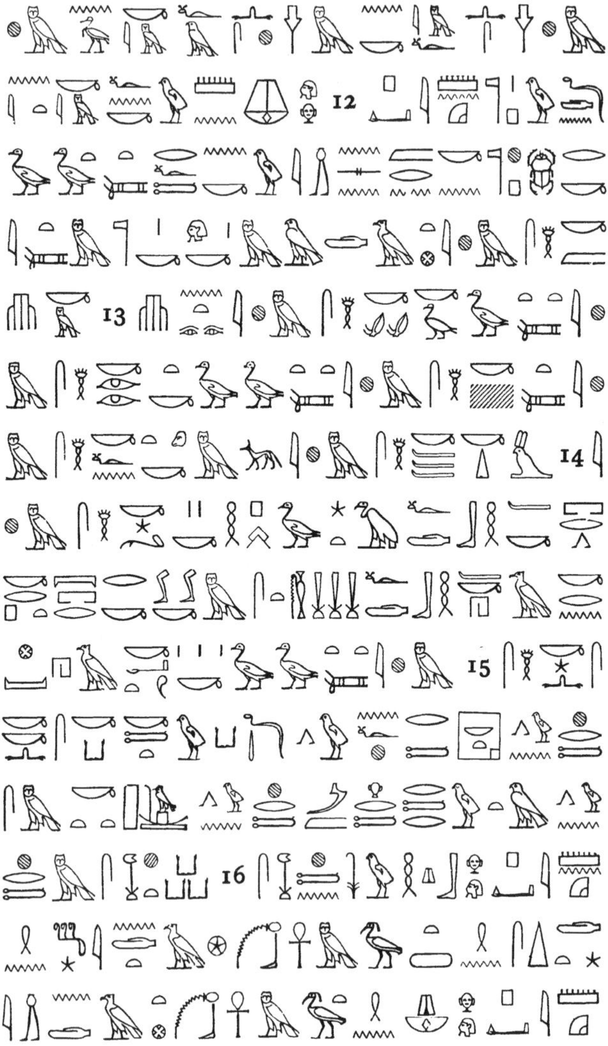

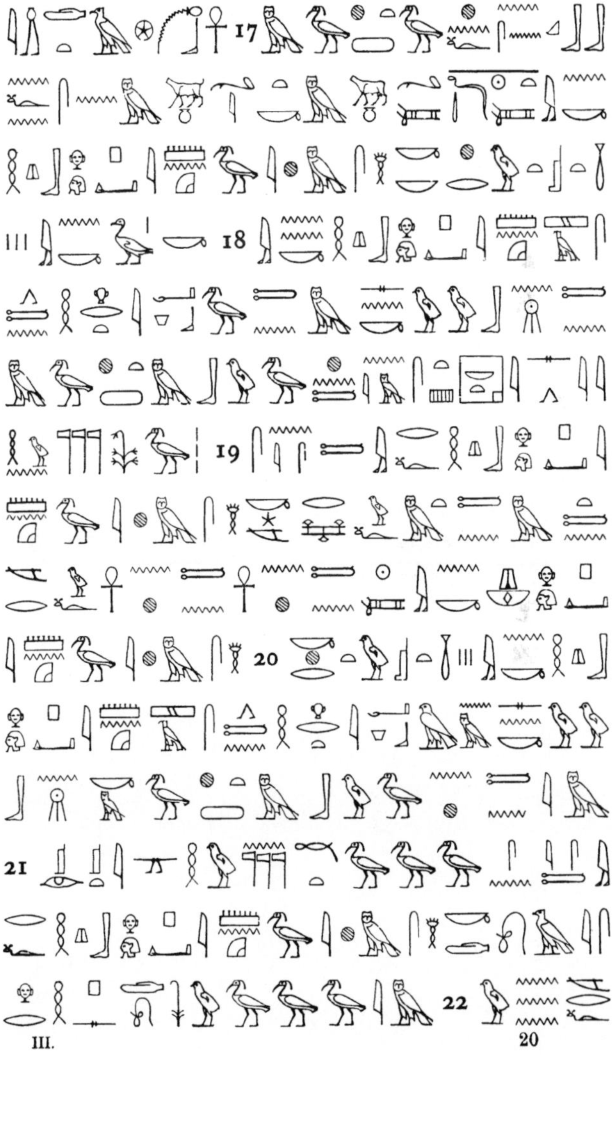

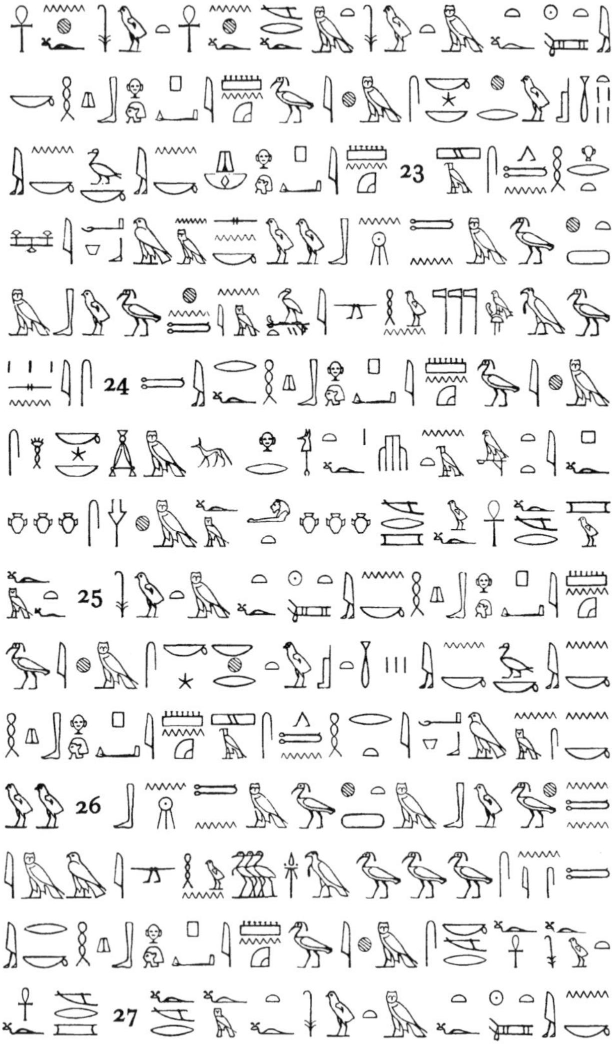
23
24
25
26
27

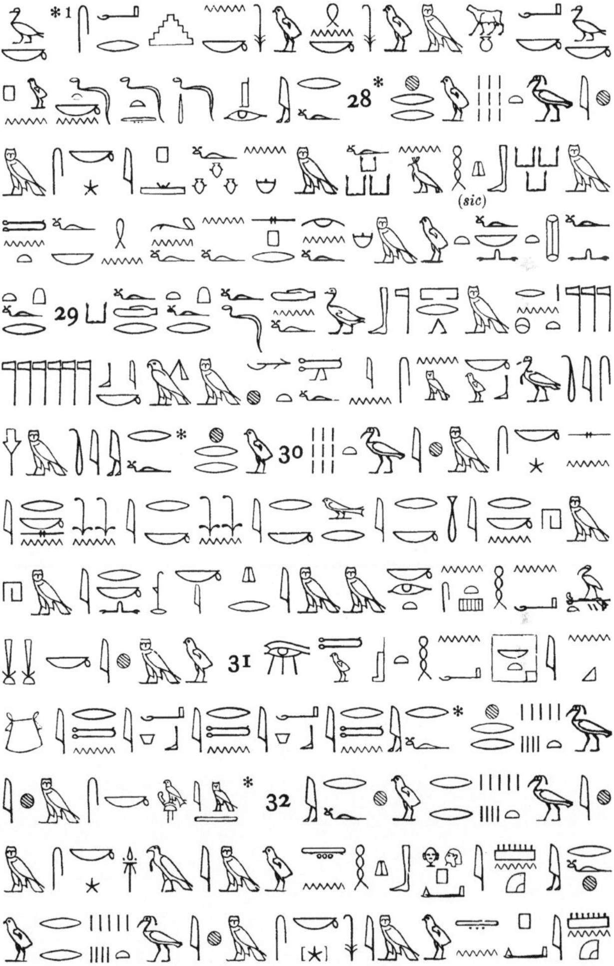

1. Here and elsewhere the asterisk indicates that the title and name of the deceased have been omitted.

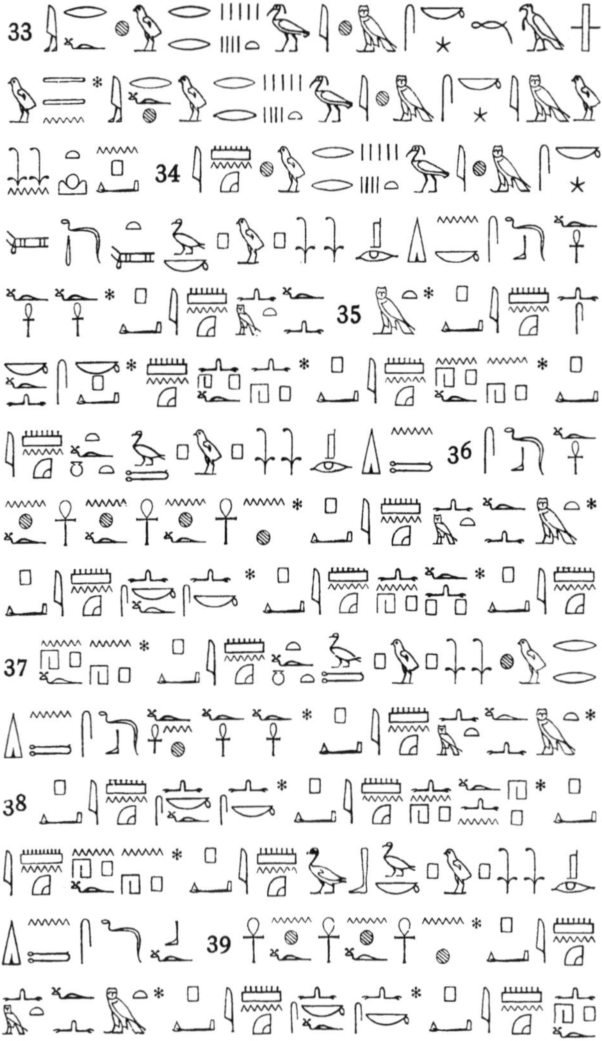

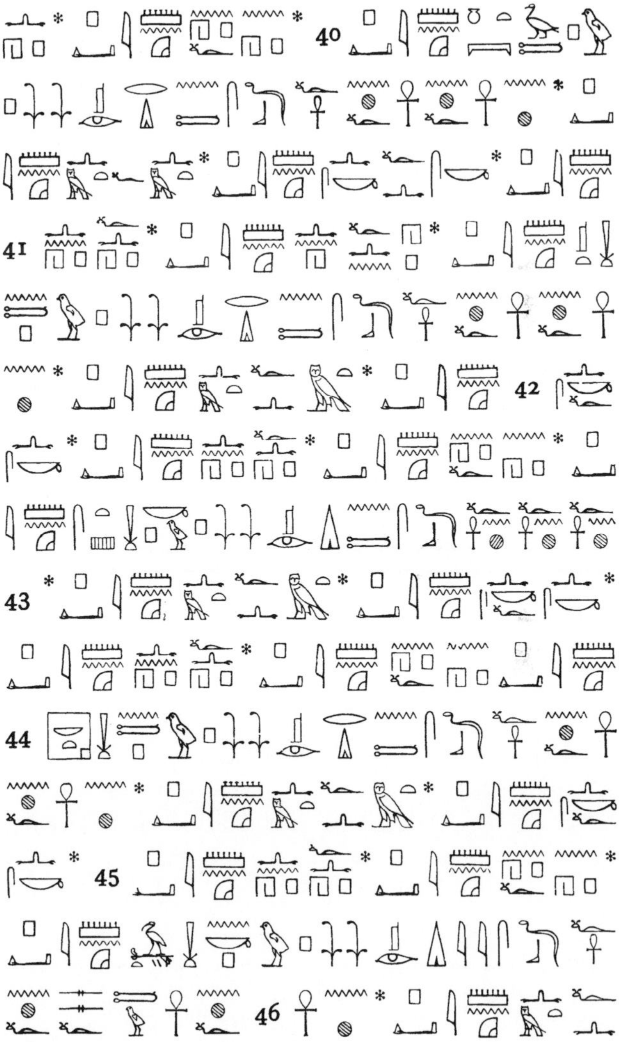
40
41
42
43
44
45
46

47
48
49
50
51
52
53

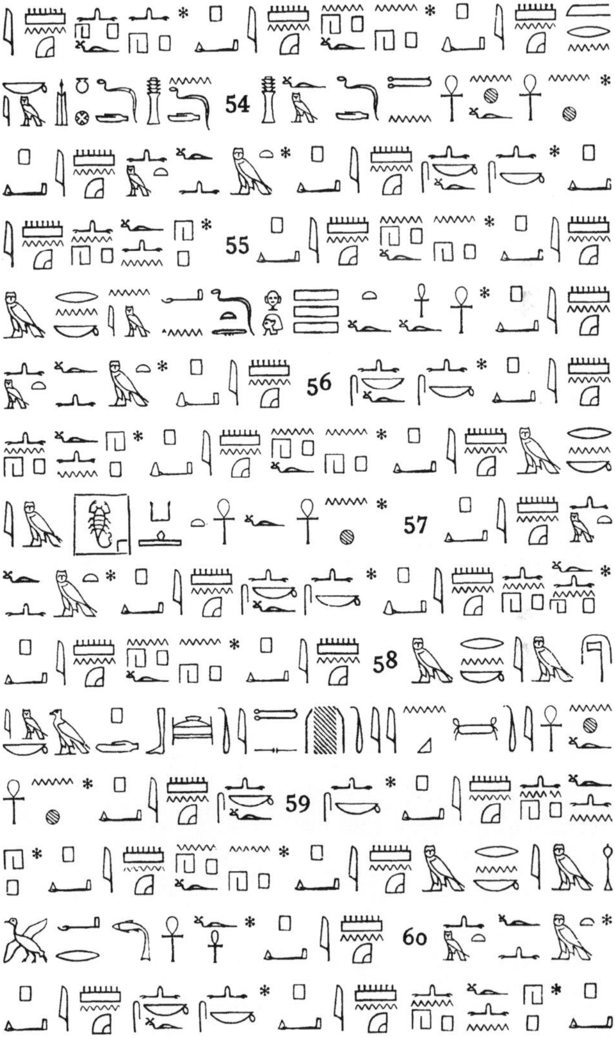

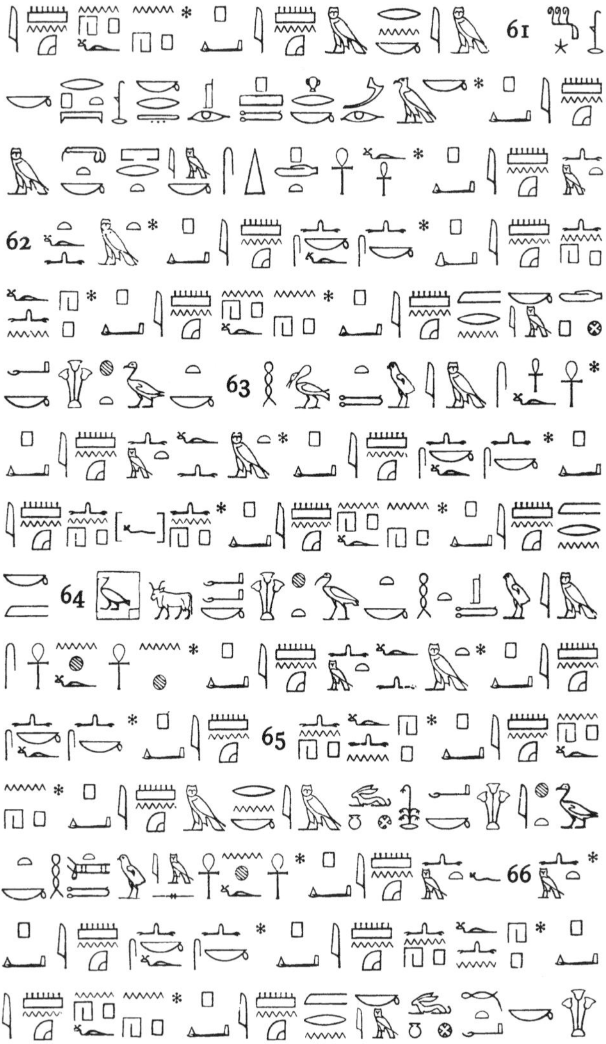
61
62
63
64
65
66

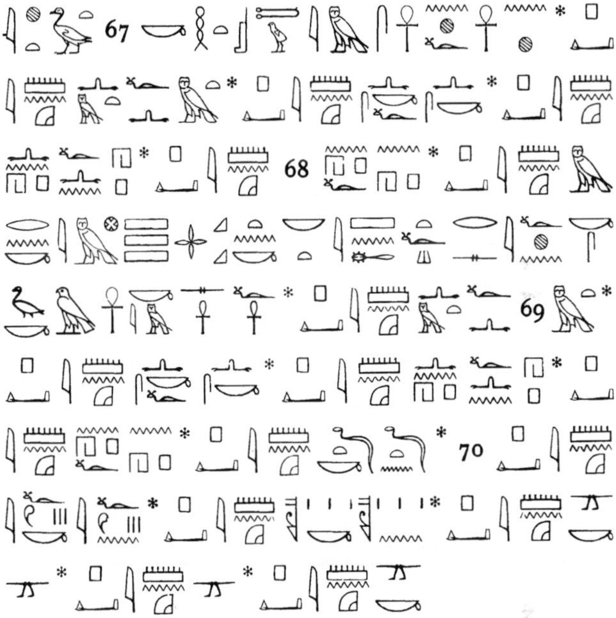

End of Volume III.

9781138567252
Reprint of #876384 - C0 - 203/127/17 - PB - Lamination Gloss - Printed on 01-Feb-19 16:00